Stand Out!!

Stand Out!!

The Secrets of Branding for a New Generation

Brian McGurk

BUSINESS EXPERT PRESS

Leader in applied, concise business books

Stand Out!!: The Secrets of Branding for a New Generation

Copyright © Business Expert Press, LLC, 2022.

Cover design by BrandCreate Ltd, Dublin, Ireland

Interior design by Exeter Premedia Services Private Ltd., Chennai, India

First published in 2021 by
Business Expert Press, LLC
222 East 46th Street, New York, NY 10017
www.businessexpertpress.com

ISBN-13: 978-1-63742-123-9 (paperback)
ISBN-13: 978-1-63742-124-6 (e-book)

Business Expert Press Digital and Social Media Marketing and Advertising Collection

Collection ISSN: 2333-8822 (print)
Collection ISSN: 2333-8830 (electronic)

First edition: 2021

10 9 8 7 6 5 4 3 2 1

To begin with…

Corporate culture is the commitment, over time, of people to the brand.

Gen B includes those born on or after the year 2000. These are the "true millennials."

Strong brands play a significant role in driving business performance. Valuing a brand is ultimately an accounting exercise.

For brand believers everywhere. May you become brand champions and brand innovators, knowing the joy of creative expression.

Description

Drawing on three decades of professional experience, this book brings the reader down less traveled paths in the world of branding, challenging current paradigms, uncovering the secrets of brand success, and introducing *Generation B*—the true millennials who are today's generation of brand natives. In addition, among its key areas of focus, *Stand Out!!* reviews the roots of financial brand valuation, explains its rationale, and explores the conditions for brand value growth, introducing the reader to a range of popular valuation methods and broader measurement approaches. The specific forces challenging brand strategy planning today are discussed in the context of a new world order of diversifying social media platforms and integrated, synchronized, personalized communication. In light of this, *Stand Out!!* makes the case for ongoing brand stewardship in the life of an organization and concludes with a focus on brand leadership and the key principles, truths, and challenges that influence brand growth and represent governing guidelines for the journey to brand success. This book is a key reference text for anyone interested in brand development, leadership, innovation, and sustainable business growth. Reader understanding and enjoyment are enhanced by ample presentation of supporting tables, charts, case examples, expert tips, real-life experiences, and pull-out quotes, as well as a helpful *word wizard* glossary at the end of each chapter explaining business terms and expressions used.

Keywords

brand; branding; brand valuation; brand strategy; millennials; Gen Z; employer branding; brand identity; brand culture; social media; digital marketing; brand communication; living the brand; brand development; brand equity; brand values; creativity; design; brand experience; brand image; brand implementation; brand leadership; brand performance; brand planning; brand principles; brand proposition; iPhone; qualitative research; talent retention

Contents

Foreword

Throughout my working life, I have always seen the word *Brand* bandied about as if it was merely a promotional tool to help drive sales. While it is true that one of the critical outputs of a good brand is its power of promotion, there are far too many instances where the brand is largely misunderstood and as a result completely under-valued. *Stand Out!!* tackles this challenge head-on, putting Brand in perspective both as a transformational strategy and as a financial and asset-building opportunity. A key strategic instrument that can unlock vision, clarify position, ensure distinction and provide a template and roadmap to sustainable growth, Brand is nevertheless often relegated to being a subset of a marketing department. What I would like to see is Brand being no less than a core part of the C-Suite armory, where it is the CEO who is the real brand manager, who has done the hard work of understanding what the brand stands for and has put together a compelling proposition that will fuel growth and capture long-term sustainable value for the shareholders. Indeed, I would argue that the brand *always* belongs in the Boardroom, as it is the Board's job to protect the assets of the firm as well as providing direction to the management team on behalf of shareholders and stakeholders.

There aren't enough published pieces on Brand as a strategic tool for the Boardroom, but Brian McGurk's excellent publication—part two of an exciting series of books under the "*Stand Out*" banner—is a groundbreaking contribution to the body of business literature in this area and is both an essential and easy read. There are many remarkable things about this book, especially its richness of ideas, useful tools, author anecdotes and the ease with which it can be read and referenced. But what is particularly special is how far it goes beyond the surface and into new territories of thinking as it probes the critical levers of strong brand building for what the author calls *today's generation of brand natives*. Critically, and in times of great challenge for talent, *Stand Out!!* pays a lot of attention to the role of culture in brand building. Talent is certain to be the greatest resource battleground of the 21st Century, and it will be those organizations with the most coherent brand promise and experience, internally as much as externally, that will gain a real competitive advantage by attracting the very best people.

And if we are really bringing Brand into the Boardroom or the C-Suite, then it has to have a level of accountability. *Stand Out!!* dives into the sources of brand valuation, proposing a number of key models to help make the intangible somewhat more tangible, while deepening understanding and alignment across different constituencies within the organization. Some years back, Paul Polman, in his strategic vision for Unilever (Unilever's Sustainable Living Plan), pointed out that Unilever had physical assets then worth €25bn but with a market cap north of €120bn, clearly demonstrating the power of brands in building enormous equity and asset value. Similarly, when Lou Gerstner took over a broken and fragmented IBM, it was through the lens of the brand that he managed to pull the company together and provide a compelling vision for alignment and growth—IBM went from bust to boom on the New York Stock Exchange. Equally, it was my own company, WPP, that looked to its brand at a time when it had gone from global dominance to a flagging share price and a loss of distinctive relevance as marketing service companies learned to both compete and collaborate with the major technology providers. A new proposition was formulated that would ultimately pull more than 130,000 employees and 3,000 companies together to form a *creative transformation company.* Thanks to greater clarity around the WPP brand and, closely related to this, a culture that is now significantly stronger, unified and more purposeful, company revenues are growing again and our share price is returning to reflect its real value. A testament indeed to the importance and power of putting the focus back on the brand.

Brian McGurk's excellent book explores these themes and more, and is simply *a must-read* as we continue to evolve our businesses and our brands in this dynamic and challenging digital age. Whether starting out on a new brand adventure or as part of a global ecosystem, *Stand*

Out!! provides the language, guides, templates, definitions, critical steps, knowledge and insights to help us leaders and learners navigate our way through and to our own next chapter.

JP Donnelly
Country Manager
WPP in Ireland
Dublin
September 24, 2021

Acknowledgments

To those who have inspired me and conspired with me to create great brands. And to those who insisted I document my insights and learnings, secrets and lessons for a wider audience.

In particular, to Róisín Griffiths and Janet French to whom I am eternally grateful for meticulous manuscript readings and for cajoling me to keep at it and keep pushing boundaries.

Finally, to my partners in publishing at Business Expert Press... for your unstinting encouragement, and for keeping the faith.

Introduction

Branding is commonly regarded as the preserve of design and in particular logo design. It is not. I confront this myopic perspective directly in my first book *Stand Out! Building Brilliant Brands for the World We Live In* where I unfold the *why do* and *how to* of branding, its evolution, philosophy, principles, and processes. The book you are now reading is different: it complements the former by exploring broader, less traveled territories of the brand domain, by identifying and defining today's generation of brand natives, by venturing into the murky world of brand valuation, and by presenting lessons, learnings, and indeed secrets drawn from three decades of branding and marketing practice. In short, this book moves the dial well away from the predilection of branding as a design-focused discipline and delves into the realms of accounting for brand value growth and the social integration of brands as shapers and identifiers of a new generation.

In the field of business management, branding is a relatively young discipline. Indeed, the first generally accepted corporate brand valuation (of Rank Hovis McDougall) took place as recently as 1988. This conveniently date-stamps the specific moment in time that there was professional recognition of brands as identifiable and quantifiable value-generating assets; it made concrete the commercial realization that *tangible* assets are, in fact, only *part* of the business valuation equation.

My hope is that *Stand Out!!* will widen perspectives, broaden horizons, and deepen understanding of the fuller reach and truly diverse nature of the field of branding, and that the reader will come away feeling encouraged, empowered, and enabled to consider, plan, and implement a wider panoply of brand development priorities, programs, and possibilities than previously considered achievable.

Brian McGurk
Dublin
September 15, 2021

CHAPTER 1

Generation B: Generation Brand

Chapter Overview

This chapter examines the legacy of generational classifications and their role in consumer understanding, preferences, and ultimately brand development. It begins with a review of the accepted generational thinking and beliefs to date and introduces Gen B as a new, more relevant classification of today's generation of *true millennials*. It highlights that brand association has developed in parallel with the rise of technology and digital innovation, and that as brand experience has become the new norm, this has nurtured a new generation of brand natives, seekers, adopters, believers. The chapter identifies the smartphone as an icon of the Gen B era and reviews the history of the rise of the mobile phone and its effect on the democratization of communications. The core demographics of Gen B are discussed and the reasons for their brand affinity expressed. In view of these insights, the nature of societal change that can be achieved by Generation B is contemplated, potentially constituting no less than a new world paradigm of enterprise values and community-centric organizational cultures.

Gen B and the Rise of the Brand Generation

Which *generation* are you? Baby Boomer, Generation X, Generation Y, Generation Z? Other? Whichever generation category you slot yourself into is deemed to indicate the factors and influences affecting your formation as a person, a citizen, and a consumer. Generational segmentation has been developed to categorize people worldwide according to their birthdate on the basis that, similar to an astrological zodiac sign, you are thereby characterized by certain attitudes, preferences, experiences, and potentialities. At the time of writing, the most recent, globally endorsed of these generational classifications remains *Gen Z*—Generation Z.

This is powerful stuff—it's therefore important to know what *generation* your customers fit into because it is believed that that will ascribe distinguishing factors that influence their lives and preferences. Having said that, a note of context and caution is warranted concerning how rigidly we both understand and date-stamp these defined *generations.* Douglas Coupland, the author of the original, seminal novel *Generation X* (1992), whose writing is widely credited with instigating this phenomenon of generational awareness and profiling, was, from the outset, loudly accusatory of marketers' misunderstanding and reinterpreting of what he had named Generation X. To clarify: in 1992, Coupland published his book *Generation X*, which is about three strangers who decide to pull back from society and move to the fringe of Palm Springs, California, to work in dreary jobs and relocate their individual identities and search for meaning. A mere three years after publishing his book, Coupland had this to say: "And now I'm here to say that X is over. I'd like to declare a moratorium on all the noise, because the notion that there now exists a different generation—X, Y, K, whatever—is no longer debatable … and the media refers to anyone aged thirteen to thirty-nine as Xers. Which is only further proof that marketers and journalists never understood that X is a term that defines not a chronological age but a way of looking at the world" (*Generation X'd, Details Magazine*, June 1995). Notwithstanding Coupland's reproach, and with the aforementioned caveat in mind, generational classifications nevertheless proved irresistible, insightful, and *de rigueur* for marketing and brand planners alike. A new framework for understanding and anticipating consumers' needs and nuances had suddenly become established and universally accepted.

When we look at the periods relating to these globally endorsed classifications, we see that the most recent adult cohort, Generation Z, stretches right back to the mid-1990s. There remains, however, little consensus among marketers and others as to precisely which years to allocate to each generational classification. In *Encyclopedia of Identity* (Jackson et al. 2010), contributing author Deric M. Greene acknowledges this, emphasizing that much debate exists on the specific timeframes defining the periods in which these generational cohorts were born. Nevertheless, each era can usefully be time-defined as follows, albeit, I admit, possessing soft start and end dates. Table 1.1 shows the general thinking relating to the relevant years attributable post-World War II to these globally accepted classifications:

Table 1.1 Post-World War II generational classifications

Classification	Years of birth	Comparative range
Baby Boomers	1946 to 1964	Mid-1940s to Mid-1960s
Generation X	1965 to 1976	Mid-1960s to Mid-1970s
Generation Y	1977 to 1996	Mid-1970s to Mid-1990s
Generation Z	1997 to date	Mid-1990s+

What has happened to marketing classifications post-90s/00s (the noughties!) you might rightly ask. This is a good question. Surely after some 25 years of living with Generation Z—and particularly given the mind-boggling rate of exponential change in these intervening years—it must or should be time for a whole new review—a global generational rethink. I believe it is. Some attempts have been made, such as Australian social analyst Mark McCrindle's *Generation Alpha*, but I propose that the current age—post-2000—be attributed more relevantly to what I call Generation B denoting *Generation Brand*. Not only, therefore, does *"Gen B"* greatly overlap *Gen Z* in terms of attributable time period, but it supersedes it. I propose Gen B as the current generational classification. But before we explore my rationale for Generation B, let's first briefly summarize the thinking behind the previous eras of Generations X, Y, and Z.

Generation X

Born during the mid-1960s to mid-1970s, Generation X experienced shifting societal values internationally, as reflected in increased participation by mothers in the workforce as well as generally absent or divorced parents—the consequence of this being that children grew up with greatly reduced adult supervision (*Demographic Profile – America's Gen X*, MetLife, 2013). Added to this, with the launch of MTV (in August 1981),

Gen X were much more market-savvy, growing up during the explosion in the music video industry accompanied by mass-media marketing and "with a front-door-key in their pocket." As a result, as young adults, they have been generally described as being laid-back slackers, cynical, and disaffected, as well as being market-savvy. Ironically, on reaching mid-life, they were found to be smart, active, happy, hard-workers who were entre-preneurial in nature and achievers of a good work–life balance. Good on them, and so much for the nay-sayers!

Generation Y

Born during the mid-1970s to the mid-1990s, Generation Y are also referred to as *millennials* as the majority of their birth cohort *reached early maturity* by the year 2000—by the new millennium. They are also known as *echo boomers* because they are the offspring of parents who were born during the postwar baby boom period (mid-1940s to mid-1960s). The thing that mostly marks out *Gen Y* is technology—they grew up with technology in a way that previous generations didn't, and with constant access to the fruits and power of the micro-chip, computers, gaming con-soles, and early-stage mobile phones. Writing in 2000, just post the Gen Y era, Howe et al. in *Millennials Rising: The Next Great Generation*, declared that "As a group, Millennials are unlike any other generation in living memory. They are more numerous, more affluent, better educated, and more ethnically diverse. More importantly, they are beginning to man-ifest a wide array of positive social habits ... including a new focus on teamwork, achievement, modesty, and good conduct." And, the author continues, "Only a few years from now, this can-do youth revolution will overwhelm the cynics and pessimists. Over the next decade, the Millennial Generation will entirely recast the image of youth from down-beat and alienated to upbeat and engaged." A positive forecast indeed, fizzing with hope and expectation, which seems to broadly align with the same author's analysis, a whole decade-and-a-half later when millennials were the next generation of incoming young–adult employees. In *Benefits Quarterly* (2014), Howe now states that "Recession-strapped young work-ers are taking a conservative new approach to financial, medical and other life risks" and went on to explain that "This new approach, in turn, grows out of a greater aversion to personal risk-taking and a greater inclination to plan for the future that Millennials first began showing earlier in life as college-age youth, as teens and even as children." And, he adamantly continues "these aren't the only new generational perspectives that Millennials are bringing to the table. Across the board, from K-12 schools to colleges and now to the workplace, Millennials have brought with them a very different set of attitudes and behaviors compared to the youth who preceded them. That includes not just risk aversion, but also a preference for group consensus, conventional aspirations ... , confidence in their future success, an insistent need for feedback and mentoring, and a collective self-image as special and as worthy of protection." Quite a CV!

Generation Z

Being born anytime from the mid-1990s places a person in the current accepted demographic classification that persists today: Generation Z. *Gen Z* is again closely identified with technology, but this time, specifically with the Internet, being the first generation to be *hands-on* with Internet usage and mobile communications from an early age. Technology, digital interaction, widespread mobile connectivity, and social media activity are a natural part of this generation's life experience, social engagement style, and peer group communication. As McCrindle defines them in *The ABC of XYZ* (2014), "Generation Z are the most materially endowed, technologically saturated, globally connected, formally educated generation our world has ever seen. For Generation Z, coming of age in the 21st Century has given them a unique perspective—having been shaped in uncertain economic times with the Global Financial Crisis, whilst also being internationally connected and engaged through global brands and global technologies."

For those growing up in this current Gen Z era, *digital* has always been around, at hand and always-on. This is the generation of the smartphone, the flatscreen, and of course, superfast broadband. How did we ever live without it? The phone in the pocket has replaced the watch on the arm. The whole world is viewed looking up through a phone camera lens or looking down through a mini flatscreen. Connectivity and social media are fab, online bullying and cyber phishing are fearful. It is a world of new exciting socialization and community formation. It is a world of frightening personal anxieties and vulnerabilities. The fears and phobias, which arise from operating in today's digital maze, were previously unknown, and a new era of cyber bullying and cybercrime has taken more than its toll on young vulnerable people and on corporate business respectively. The power, opportunities, and threats of smart technology and mobile communication is nowhere more evident than in the rise of online social communities and personal peer groups. But, also in this space, and because of the social power of mobile social media platforms and peer group identification, brands have come to the fore, recognizing and responding to the new means of communication, the new technologies, the new demands and desires of a new always-on smartphone generation. This generation is what I call Generation B—Generation Brand. And, here's why.

Introducing Generation B

To a large extent, the fixation of the last decades' generational demographic classifications has been narrowly on technology and digital development and its impact on personal communications. This fixation with the transformative, emotive, and addictive power of technology has distracted from a parallel development that has been taking place in brand positioning and values-association. In broad terms, as presented in Table 1.2, it could be said that, internationally, the war years—the late 1930s and 1940s—were preoccupied with manufacturing (most notably armaments and heavy equipment), the postwar years—the 1950s and 1960s—elevated selling as a professional process, the 1970s and 1980s were intent on formalizing marketing as the new strategic discipline, with the 1990s, noughties, and postmillennial period witnessing the primacy of brand as a transformative, profit-generating strategy.

In *A Short History of Business and Entrepreneurial Evolution during the 20th Century: Trends for the New Millennium*, Hunter (2013) puts in valuable chronological context these changes in the key drivers of business focus and strategy from post-World War II to the new millennium. In doing so, the author maintains that the period of production orientation actually endured for multiple decades, stating that: "Right into the 1960s most companies in America were production orientated, seeing the market

Table 1.2 The change in primary drivers of business growth over time

Designated period of development	Primary driver of development
1930s to 1940s	Manufacturing
1950s to 1960s	Selling
1970s to 1980s	Marketing
1990s to 2000s	Branding

as the means to dispose of their production." Intriguingly, he also high-lights that there was, at the same time, a widespread awakening happening regarding the importance of putting a concerted focus on the customer, with this culminating in Theodore Levitt's argument, as Hunter restates it, that "companies should become much more customer orientated in their approach to the market." Nevertheless, Hunter emphasizes the seri-ous lead-time that persisted here between marketing thought and action, lamenting the fact that "Although Levitt's ideas were accepted by corporate America in the 1960s, *it was not until the 1980s* that the marketing revolu-tion came to fruition (whereupon) marketing departments began growing and the marketing manager became a powerful driver of the company."

The knock-on effect of this delay in marketing orientation was deeply felt by the 1970s. As Hunter continues: "Until the 1970s, American business had been competing among themselves with a great deal of predictability (whereupon) Japanese companies employed very precise marketing prac-tices at a time when American manufacturers thought they knew everything about marketing. Japanese companies were to employ their style of market selection, market entry, market penetration, and market maintenance that made American executives ponder about this new Japanese success."

Subsequently, post the 1980s, a sea-change: brand philosophy took center-stage and brands prospered, but did so under the glare of the tech-nology boom. People were somewhat blinded by the speed of technolog-ical change and exciting new techy product offerings. They were buying the dream promised by fast technological progress and innovative prod-ucts but were not actually sure how to fully integrate these into their daily lives and work practices or indeed how to live the dream that technology essentially offered (and still does). While the fantastic achievements of micro-chip-based technology, data processing, and mobile connectivity have been a marvel to behold, it is not only processing speed, design aesthetics, or product lightness that have delivered the wow—the establishment of global technology brands and the promotion of their brand meaning and personality has also left us breathless.

Brands are about dreams—and linked to technological innovation, brands offer huge consumer promise and create massive consumer emotion. And so came the rise of the technology brands: Apple, Intel, Dell, Samsung, Sony, HP, Microsoft, and so on. At time of writing, the number one technology brand, Apple, is the most valuable company and brand in the world. So, with the rise of technology and digital innovation came the tech, IT, and digital company and product brands. But, brands didn't stop there. In parallel to developments in the tech sector, brands were and are transforming buyer, shopper, and consumer experiences and lives globally. Brands have come of age, and indeed, the appreciation for, acceptance of, and association with brands and brand experiences in our daily lives mark out the present generation of consumers as being *the brand generation*. This generation—Gen B—lives in a branded world, where brand is king and, more, where brand is understood as a maker of self-image, a driver of self-esteem, a proof of discernment, a facilitator of communication, a passport to peer groups, a proof of quality, a portrayer of values, a sign of taste, an expression of personality, even a mark of intelligence.

Generation B comprises all those who have grown up in this brand generation and who, therefore, value brands and prefer them for numerous reasons, be they reasons of quality, function, emotion, personality, or social or peer group identification. People these days choose brands for the dream, for the brand community, for the brand associations, for the performance, for the value for money. This was not generally so until the final decade of the last millennium and has now become deeply engrained in our current new-millennial consumer psychology and everyday buying behavior—whether we are aware of it or not. So, from my perspective, I see Gen B as including those who were born on and after the year 2000. I call these the *true millennials* because they were actually born at and from the very beginning of the new millennium and became brand-aware and brand-savvy from early childhood.

Gen B includes those born on and after the year 2000. I call these the "true millennials."

From Mobile Phone to Smartphone: An Icon of the Gen B Era

An icon of the Gen B era is the rise of the smartphone, and the evolution of the smartphone is symptomatic of the era in which Gen B has come to maturity. A review of the history here, as summarized in Table 1.3, provides interesting and relevant context.

Motorola was the first company to produce a handheld mobile phone and, on April 3, 1973, Martin Cooper, a Motorola researcher and executive, made the first mobile telephone call from handheld subscriber equipment in midtown Manhattan, placing a call to his rival Dr. Joel S. Engel in Bell Labs, New Jersey. Ten years later, in 1983, the first mobile phones were marketed to the general public by Motorola, but the first true smartphone didn't make its debut until 1992 and the actual term *smartphone* didn't come into public usage until 1995. The first genuine smartphone was created by IBM and was unveiled on November 2, 1992—this was the Simon Personal Communicator. The first Apple iPhone was released almost 15 years later on June 29, 2007. The launch of the iPhone was historic, as it offered a whole new intuitive approach to accessing and interacting with mobile telephony while exploiting the capability and benefits of digital connectivity.

Like the creation of the first mobile phone in 1973, the launch of the first iPhone marks an historic moment, a tipping point, between the past and the future. Why? Because, as Gershon reminds us: "The iPhone was the first all-in-one integrated cell phone that combines

Table 1.3 From mobile phone to smart phone: key historical landmarks

Innovation	Change agent(*)	Date/timing
1st mobile phone call	Motorola (Martin Cooper)	April 3, 1973
1st mobile phone unveiled prior to marketing	Motorola (DynaTAC 8000X)	March 6, 1983
1st mobile phone sold (Midwest/East coast USA)	DynaTAC 8000X / $3,995	March 13, 1984
1st *smartphone* debuted	IBM (Simon Personal Communicator/$900)	November 2, 1992
1st iPhone released	Apple Inc (iPhone 2G/$600)	June 29, 2007

(*) Cost at time of product debut as quoted by Ooma Inc.

voice communication, internet access, and music and photo storage. The iPhone set the standard for future smartphone design" *Digital Media and Innovation: Management and Design Strategies in Communication* (Gershon 2017).

The smartphone—and particularly the iPhone—has had vast ramifications on modern communications, digital interactivity, marketing strategies, and socialization. It has, in short, enabled and ushered in the democratization of communications via telephony, messaging, social media usage, and personal connectivity—or as Gershon goes on to say: "The iPhone fundamentally changed how people communicate and interact with the world. To that end, Apple has created an entire digital media ecosystem." And, although an iconic creation of the Generation B era, it now resides in the hands of all generations regardless of age, occupation, or geography.

In an important sense, the smartphone represents the convergence of technology, design, and marketing—all key components of a modern-day brand experience. As such, it drew on the power of branding to deliver a unique and outstanding experience while also benefiting branding by becoming an exceptional example of the establishment of a world-changing new brand category.

While the iPhone was the first true smartphone groundbreaker, and has innovated continuously ever since its launch in 2007, there have been and are many innovative competitors, impressive product alternatives, and consequently, a wide array of product models and options to choose from in the burgeoning smartphone market today. In these circumstances, brand competition becomes rife, with the successful brands thriving on such dynamic change and choice. Above all, brands in these fast-paced technological markets ring the changes from one technological breakthrough to another as players invest, innovate, and reposition their product offerings to outmaneuver competitors as they anticipate future consumer requirements and desires. Nevertheless, the iPhone, although experiencing tough and challenging competition today, marks a high point in the early years of this millennium and in the life experience, perspective, and expectations of its Generation B cohort.

Let's now explore a little more the personalia and demographics of the Gen B market audience. Generation B, born in and since the year 2000, comprises the full spectrum of today's teenage and early adult cohort—spanning, at time of writing, from 13 to 21 years of age.

Core characterizations of this (mainly teenager-based) youth cohort are: Today's teens—Gen B—have not so much adopted social media as their own but have been born into it and claimed rightful ownership of it. This heady mixture of digital connectivity and teenage angst has undoubtedly caused stress not only in the experience of the Gen B cohort itself but across all strata of society as a whole. Nevertheless, it would be more than myopic not to be impressed—if not amazed—at the speed of digital change that has occurred and to accept that change happens, is inevitable, is good and its goodness must be recognized and adopted. Gen B have done just this. They are as one with things digital, embracing of technology, engaged by social media, committed to connectivity. They are the always-on generation, and this is the always-on age. They are also the brand generation. By virtue of the fact that they are the teenage set, they are as ever the most self-conscious of all societal groups, the most self-aware, and the most sensitive to image and to product attributes and brand associations. In *Teenagers' Purposive Brand Relationships*, Aledin (2012) declares that "Teenagers use their brands in a purposive manner; they help master their daily social interaction, seek connectedness and acceptance as well as deal with their self-esteem" and concludes that "Brands are relationship partners (for teenagers) … they help them to express and construct their identities, and give them confidence in the exciting and insecure search for a balance between fitting in and standing out." Teenagers are on a mission in this generation—as of course in previous—to fit in with the crowd, to be one of the group, to identify with social peers, to personally express but within the parameters of social norms for their teenage peer group. Brands provide this access to peer group identification today in a way that maybe music alone did in the past.

Brands are permission, they are proof, they are access. As brands have become more center-stage in personal expression and consumer experience, everyone has reached out to them, in recognition of their values, for affirmation, to strengthen self-esteem, to make a personal or corporate statement, none more so than Generation B, the present teenage demographic.

Brands are permission, they are proof, they are access.

While today, straddling right across the teenage years—a wide span of ages and degrees of maturity—Gen B is characterized as being both *social media savvy* and *brand savvy*. Whether it be techy toys and games for Gen B's early teens' cohort, or clothing, cosmetics, and protein shakes for the late teens, what you consume, what you wear, and what you associate with is at least as important, even more so, than the functional attributes or performance of any particular product or service adopted. Figure 1.1 summarizes key Gen B profile characteristics and personal priorities.

Generation B are big-time into social reputation, sense-checking their peers, keeping up with the trends and keeping in with friends—their prime influencers and age cohort. Brands are built to interpret and

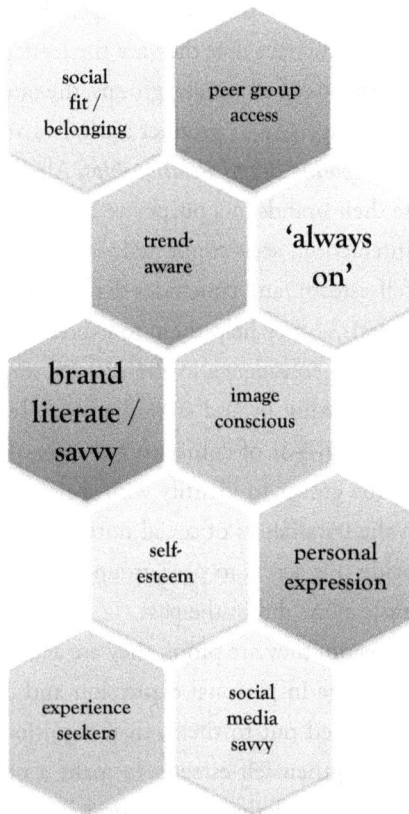

Figure 1.1 Gen B—profile characteristics and priorities

express such personal desires, to convey such social fit, to speak the language of the audience.

In a sense, brands were, so to speak, *made* for this primarily teenage demographic, and although, of course, brands (different ones) are created for, and adopted widely by, all generations and audiences, the need for understanding and expression in the sensitive, pressured, searching, need-for-belonging teenage years makes for a particularly powerful and symbiotic personal relationship.

It will be fascinating to see how Generation B develops in its brand relationships as it ages and matures, and how it will leverage, integrate, and drive innovation in brands as this demographic cohort takes on roles and responsibilities for societal development and social formation in the years and decades ahead.

Projecting forward, it is likely that Generation B will increasingly bring classic brand values to the fore and center of society as, in time, they take over responsibility for societal leadership. They are likely to greatly accelerate the ongoing transformation of global and national society from a traditional coercive power-based paradigm to one that is based on values of trust, openness, connectivity, personal fulfillment, innovation, reward, ethics, sustainability, equality, and creativity. As Britton (2015) proclaims in *YouthNation: Building Remarkable Brands in a Youth-Driven Culture*, "For brands today, the old marketing models are over. The status quo is dead. Today's rapidly shifting marketplace requires businesses to be agile, connected, authentic, artful, meaningful, immersive, and socially responsible."

As reflected in Figure 1.2, community (enabled by connectivity) is likely to be a prime tenet of the future Gen B-led business organization, which I forecast will exhibit a confidence in creativity and ingenuity engendered in a culture of trust and care for people, planet, and product. In his book *The Future of Work*, Morgan (2014) endorses people-centric change, envisioning that a normative sea-change is called for in the relationship between employees, managers, and organizations. He maintains that and he anticipates that priorities have to change from a profit-driven to a prosperity-driven metric of success. "The future employee," he declares, "wants to work for an organization that believes and invests in sustainability and community development, corporate social responsibility,

community /
connectivity

transparency
/ openness

personal
reward

equality

creativity /
ingenuity

sustainability

ethics
and values

care

innovation

trust

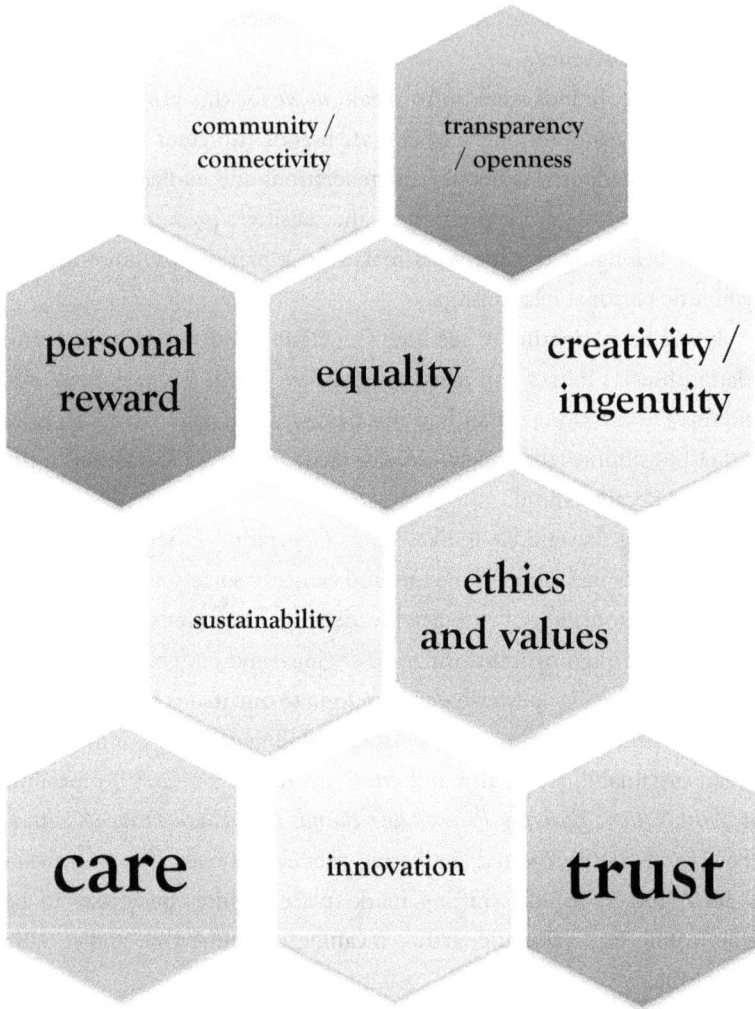

Figure 1.2 Gen B—establishing a new world paradigm

health and wellness, employee happiness, ethical choices, and in making
the world a better place." This is the expectation and frame of mind of
Gen B, and the signs of this new world paradigm are already in evidence
among brand-led companies, and more obviously those in the renowned
global tech and social media sectors such as Apple, Microsoft, Google,
Facebook, LinkedIn. Much, however, remains to be done worldwide to
inculcate, harmonize, and globalize these new cultural values, standards,
and ways of working.

The ongoing democratization of communications of the current social media era is sure to increasingly drive greater levels of transparency and corporate responsibility across all business sectors. In so doing, this will open the way for branded organizations to instill, integrate, and activate previously aspirational values to realize new ways of working and new collaborative-style work experiences. These will be founded on the prevalence of ever-more powerful mobile computing capability combined with ever-faster Internet connectivity.

Generation B are set to bring brands foursquare into play to nurture, achieve, and sustain new cultural norms and enterprise values. And, they are best placed to do so as they are the first generation to both embrace the new smart communications technologies and to integrate these seamlessly and deeply within their personal lives. In so doing, they have positioned digital connectivity and social messaging not only as the new mainstream but as the new norm of this (still) new millennium.

Key Takeaways

Gen B supersedes Gen Z as the new generation of today's postmillennial brand-aware and brand-engaged consumers.

Gen B are the *true millennials* as they were born in or after the year 2000.

Gen B marks the era of appreciation for, acceptance of, and association with brands and brand experiences in the consumer's daily life.

Technology has been a key driver of generational consumer definition: Gen X and MTV; Gen Y and the micro-chip; Gen Z and the internet; and, today, Gen B and always-on digital connectivity.

The new millennium has witnessed the uniquely transformative parallel development of digital mobile technology and values-based brand association.

The smartphone is an icon of the Gen B era, marking the convergence of technology, design, and marketing; the delivery of unique brand experience; and the democratization of communications.

People choose brands for a dream built on emotional value associations, peer group community, outstanding product performance,
and distinctive value for money.

As they take up future leadership roles, Generation B are expected to
usher in worldwide societal transformation that is emphatically
values-based. This will ultimately shift accepted organizational
norms from a power-based to a trust-based paradigm.

The Word Wizard	
Expression	**Explanation**
Attributes	Key characteristics, features, or qualities
Brand associations	The perceptions, experiences, and reputation that people associate with a brand
Brand experience	The full and combined benefits and effect in functional and emotional terms of using or consuming a brand
Brand positioning	The process of establishing or strengthening brand relevance in a defined market in order to develop and maintain a specific reputation and competitive position
Branding	The visual expression of a brand's innate idea, proposition, and uniqueness
Cultural norms	The set of standard beliefs, behaviors, or communications that characterize a societal or organizational culture
Culture	Organizational culture is the values and set of behaviors that are expressed, endorsed, and engrained among employees and suppliers. Brand culture is the commitment, over time, of people (in-company and in-market) to the brand
Democratization	Achieving full availability and open access for the general public
Demographics	Socio-economic characteristics and statistical data relating to a population and its particular subgroups
Enterprise values	The standards, ethics, and codes of conduct and behavior prioritized and committed to by a business enterprise
Functional	Physical attributes and benefits
Millennials	Also known as *Generation Y*, millennials are people born from the mid-1970s to the mid-1990s whose birth cohort had reached early maturity by the year 2000—by the new millennium
Norms	The set of standard beliefs, behaviors, or communications that characterize typical activity or normal practice

The Word Wizard	
Expression	**Explanation**
Paradigm	An accepted basic concept of theory, belief, or practice
Peer group	A primary, influencing social group of people who have similar interests, age, background, or social status
Personalia	The biographical or personal details, preferences, or concerns associated with an individual or grouping
Symbiotic relationship	A piggybacking type relationship where commercial benefits are mutually enjoyed due to collaborative sharing of vision, know-how, or market access
Values	What a brand or a business supports, promotes, and stands for as its essential ethics, priorities, and points of difference in both functional and emotional terms
Ways-of-working	Procedures and systems of internal organization that promote the development and maintenance of a companywide brand-centric culture

Experience

A revolution is in hand: I learned recently that primary school children are quickly losing their *fine motor skills*: their writing is suffering badly because of the overuse of handheld flatscreens and the underuse of pencil and paper. Ironically, there appears to be a battle between dexterity (on a smartphone or tablet) and fine motor skills (for handwriting and fine tactile work). A revolution is in hand (literally!). Gen X-ers and Gen Y-ers are under pressure to keep up with Gen Z-ers and Gen B-ers in the use of mobile technology; Gen B-ers are outstripping all others of course in the integration and use of *iTech* in their lifestyles. The gap appears to be widening with time and with the proliferation of smart software and smartphone innovations. The implications for change in our social relationships, community interdependence, and communication norms are intriguing and thought-provoking.

Expertise

Always embrace change: Change is good, and anyway it's inevitable. It was the *technology* of the fountain pen followed quickly by the ballpoint pen that put paid to the thousand-year-old quill pen (1,300 years actually!). The writing was on the wall. Resistance was futile.

And now (since 2007), the smartphone has landed! Embrace change ... or else!

Example

Old yet innovating: Rathbornes Candle-makers (1488) is Ireland's oldest manufacturing company and is one of the oldest companies in the world. Twitter is among the newest. It was established in 2006, Facebook in 2004, LinkedIn in 2002, Netflix in 1997, Yahoo in 1995, Amazon in 1994, and Apple in 1976. The oldest still-trading company in the world is Kongo Gumi (578)—a Japanese construction company that specializes in building Buddhist temples. It remained a family-run company for more than 1,400 years until it was bought over in 2006. Embracing change while innovating and building a brand reputation for excellence is something which such elder-statesman companies have obviously made into an art form. Newcomers (including tech companies) take note!

CHAPTER 2

Secrets and Lessons From the Leading Edge

Chapter Overview

Learnings, lessons, insights, and secrets are presented and explored under six headings: understanding branding, planning branding, creating branding, briefing branding, implementing branding, and internalizing branding. These detail the findings and conclusions of the hands-on consulting practitioner (me!) who has plied his creative trade at the leading-edge of business and commercial development in organizations of all sizes and diverse types. Some will smack of plain common sense, some will clarify, some will challenge, some will uncover hidden truths, some will complete your knowledge. Taken together, all will inform strategic decision making, build creative confidence, and strengthen brand performance.

The Secrets and Lessons of Successful Branding

Is there a secret to branding? Are there lessons to be learned? Having worked on branding and brand development for almost three decades, here are some of my discoveries, definitions, and descriptions that are followed by detailed discussions and explanations of each. And just one caveat—as most of my branding experience has been gleaned as a hands-on practitioner in the field of corporate consulting, the following discussion reflects this with the liberal use of the word *client* throughout the text. In some instances, such as in the section *Briefing Branding*, this is unavoidable; in other instances, I have preferred to keep faith with the word *client* (as opposed to *company* or *customer*), as I believe it brings an instructive sense of situation and authenticity, and a valuable reminder of the sharp-edged commercial reality in which these learnings, lessons, insights, and, indeed, secrets have been gathered.

Understanding Branding

1. Branding is two words not one.
2. Branding is about two things: words and images.
3. A brand can be defined in many ways. Few are one-word definitions. My two favorite one-worders are *uniqueness* and *reputation*.
4. Identity is not the same thing as image.
5. Branding is not a science; it is not an art; it is a process.
6. 75 percent of what makes a brand great has nothing to do with the product or service delivered!
7. The brand does not live in the boardroom or the managing director's (MD's) office. It lives in the marketplace.
8. Brand thinking motivates an organization and magnifies its growth potential. Without it, a business must under-exert, under-perform, and under-achieve.
9. There are three levels of brand creation: new brands, refreshed brands, rebrands.

Planning Branding

10. Don't think branding first. Think brand proposition.
11. Brand strategy is not about getting it perfect. It's about getting it together.
12. Be patient. Constructing a brand model takes a number of iterations.
13. Research till you can predict the next response.
14. Qualitative research is essential to brand understanding.
15. Make personality the rich relation.

Creating Branding

16. Make sure the creative gets the big idea, not just the written brief.
17. Aim for a strong identity. Be brave with colors and imagery.
18. Believe in the power of poetry in business. Words can sing.
19. Create the name and take the credit.

Briefing Branding

20. Clients do not buy what they do not like. Take regular soundings on identity design expectations and preferences.

21. Clients do not buy what they do not understand. Explain the brand principles, psychology, and practicality for all identity design components.

22. Do not patronize clients. Encourage *the stupid question*. They will need to understand the design strategy, visual options, and recommended solution rationale.

23. Anticipate and keep ahead of inevitable client queries. Beat them to the e-mail or the phone call.

24. Pitching for work? Inform the brief to transform your chance.

Implementing Branding

25. Under-promise and over-deliver. It's an age-old principle that has stood the test of time—a real smart strategy in the fast-moving world of a branding program.

26. Brand decision making depends not only on operational stakeholders but also political stakeholders. Engage both.

27. Brand logo is not the end-goal. External–internal brand alignment is. Your competitive market positioning depends on it.

28. Brand awareness is not enough. Brand understanding is necessary if brand behavior is to change. Brand experience is always the Holy Grail.

29. Brand implementation does not just happen. Strategy is about *the know* and communication is about *the go*. But it all starts internally.

30. Brands should be celebrated before they are calculated.

Internalizing Branding

31. Prioritize people and culture: balance brand design development with internal employer–brand investment.

32. Employees are essential: Branding's just pretty without people. But very powerful with them engaged.

33. Activate a *Living the Brand* program. Prioritize your mechanics of change.

34. Identify your instinctive internal brand champions. Use their natural passion to evangelize across the organization.

35. Recognize. Reward. Celebrate. Brand success is a communal experience without walls. Structure this into the annual calendar.

Understanding Branding

Branding Is Two Words Not One

I am always conscious that we in the branding business are dealing with two words, concepts even, which are often used interchangeably: brand and branding, or as I like to put it: Brand(ing) is two words not one!: *Brand* is the idea, and *ing* is short for communicating it. Brand(ing), therefore, means *communicating an idea.* I believe it is important to think of branding in this way because it connects the strategic idea-generating process with the design-centric creative communicating process, encompassing both these distinct disciplines, mindsets, and skillsets within the *branding* word. Otherwise, brand and branding can often be used interchangeably, resulting in confusion, lack of clarity, and misunderstanding about what precisely is being meant. Indeed, without an understanding of branding as integrating both the idea and its communication, then *branding* is more often than not regarded as merely relating to the design of a brand logo or visual identity. Understanding branding as two words not one protects the use of the word from misconstruance. The fact is that branding is both a strategic and a creative process: the communication of an idea. It is vital that it be fully understood as such.

Branding Is About Two Things: Words and Images

As mentioned elsewhere, I often say that branding is simply about two things: words and images. Simple as this may seem, the creative and business challenge comes in how to correlate, coordinate, and communicate these to do justice to the brand's strategic proposition and purpose in the marketplace. Nonetheless, it is refreshing to consider branding in such simple terms. It is reassuring to realize that confident control over the set of words and images that we apply around the business and in support of our brands will determine the cut-through of key customer messages about the proposition and values we espouse. The magic of course comes in the astute and creative interaction of visuals and copywritten messaging so as to align a brand's value proposition to the consumer's need and desire. To illustrate, Figure 2.1 shows the inevitable, sequential macro stages from brand visioning to deployment of creative elements for brand building and activation of customer cut-through. Achievement of a strong, consumer-resonating result is normally firstly dependent on the availability of a well-thought-out and confident strategy point of reference; this is usually documented in writing and stipulates the underlying guiding corporate philosophy and brand principles, values, and tone of voice which are to guide all market and brand communications. Nevertheless, and albeit requiring sound strategic thinking and leadership team consensus, branding is indeed about just two things: words and images. Select scrupulously, utilize imaginatively, apply consistently!

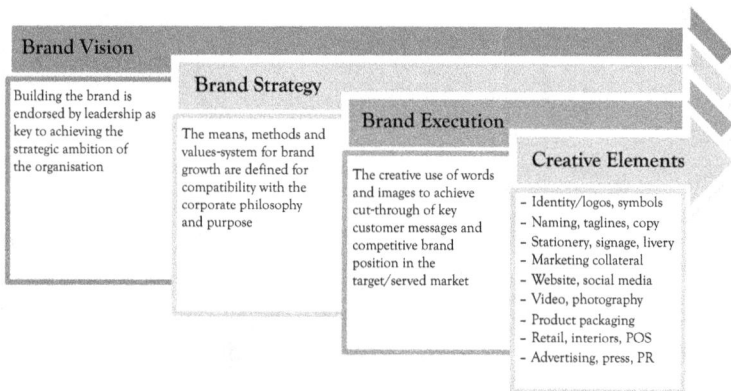

Brand Vision

Building the brand is endorsed by leadership as key to achieving the strategic ambition of the organisation

Brand Strategy

The means, methods and values-system for brand growth are defined for compatibility with the corporate philosophy and purpose

Brand Execution

The creative use of words and images to achieve cut-through of key customer messages and competitive brand position in the target/served market

Creative Elements

– Identity/logos, symbols
– Naming, taglines, copy
– Stationery, signage, livery
– Marketing collateral
– Website, social media
– Video, photography
– Product packaging
– Retail, interiors, POS
– Advertising, press, PR

Figure 2.1 From brand vision to creative execution: Activating customer cut-through

A Brand Can Be Defined in Many Ways. Few Are One-Word Definitions. My Two Favorite One-Worders Are "Uniqueness" and "Reputation"

What is a brand? This is often the title of an early slide in a brand consultant's or brand manager's presentation. The answers vary like the weather! So, it's judicious and of course challenging to try to boil it down to just a one-word handle, and this can have great merit in keeping our understanding and thinking anchored when confronted with what is otherwise a sea of alternative definitions and so often confusing, elaborate offerings. In a previous era, when marketing was an up-and-coming discipline, which had to prove its commercial worth, leading thinkers would craft up long-winded definitions, highly technical in tone, to present all things marketing as having a scientific nature. Marketing was identified as a form of commercial science, and *marketing science* was often the nomenclature attributed to it in the academic world. It was only when marketing had found its feet, so to speak, and became a mature and recognized profession, that branding as a distinct discipline was born. In many ways, branding is a child of marketing, and by the time it got fully-fledged, the world had changed. So, instead of verbose and formal communications (and definitions), branding by its nature needed to be able to express itself in more curt and snappier terms. Where verbosity was vanity, now brevity was beauty and was valued as such by modern communications practitioners. All this, of course, to be duly escalated by the arrival of digital communications and social media messaging—the era of Twitter with its original 140-character tweet restriction being a prime example. And so the long-winded was replaced by the abbreviated.

Where verbosity was vanity, now brevity was beauty.

In line with this, I have defined a brand pithily as *uniqueness you know, want, and trust*—the rationale being that there is something unique or distinct in the first place about a company, product, or service; that folks get to know about it and try it out; that they enjoy and get value from it; and in doing so, they develop trust in it and—the brand effect—they become repeat and loyal customers (and tell all their friends about it too).

So, now for a one-word definition! Reflecting the preceding, my first offer would be *uniqueness*; my second offer would be *reputation*. Therefore, a brand is your uniqueness or the point of difference that you deliver, which the customer recognizes as being personally relevant and value-adding. Alternatively, a brand is your reputation—your image in the marketplace that provides distinctiveness, competitive differentiation, and customer appeal, and which again (always!) is personally relevant and value-adding. Uniqueness? Reputation? You choose!

Identity Is Not the Same Thing as Image

Brand identity or brand image? Which is correct? Well, that depends. So often, *identity* and *image* are used interchangeably. So often, people when asked about their brand will talk about their logo—that's identity.

Whereas the more interesting and deeper response should be about perceptions: what their brand stands for in the market—that's image. They are, therefore, not the same thing! *Identity* is the visual representation of the brand, yes through its logo (or brand mark) as well as through all manifestations of its visual form across all media and communication platforms. That means that whenever, wherever, and however the brand is visually manifested is what constitutes its brand identity. A brand's identity is the universal visual expression of the brand to anyone, anywhere, anyhow be that inside or outside an organization, among staff, suppliers, customers, stakeholders, the public, and marketing media.

> *A brand's identity is the universal visual*
> *expression of the brand to anyone,*
> *anywhere, anyhow.*

The brand identity is comprised of all and every visual asset and marketing collateral (its applications) to be found inside and outside the organization. The creator of brand identity is, therefore, the designer, and specifically the graphic designer. Of course, as I often say, "branding is about two things: words and images." Simple. But the creative and business challenge come in how to correlate, coordinate, and communicate words and images to do justice to the brand's strategic proposition and purpose in the marketplace. Graphic design is clearly a key driver and creator of the visual image to be projected by the business and, in the majority of businesses, it is the driving creative force behind the brand identity. But within *design*, I would also include photography because the visual *design* of a photograph is critical to a brand's identity. In this day and age, the projected visual image is more powerful than ever, and none more so than the photograph (because as we know a picture is worth a thousand words!). The power and importance of the photograph, however, are exponentially extended and magnified in the brand video, and in an era where people look but do not read, the video *experience* has become omnipresent and *de rigeur* for any committed branded product or business. The power of the printed word, of course, is also a force to be reckoned with, but apart from important typography choices and their usage guidelines, the printed word otherwise plays a relatively minor role visually in delivering the overall brand identity stand-out and sustained market impact.

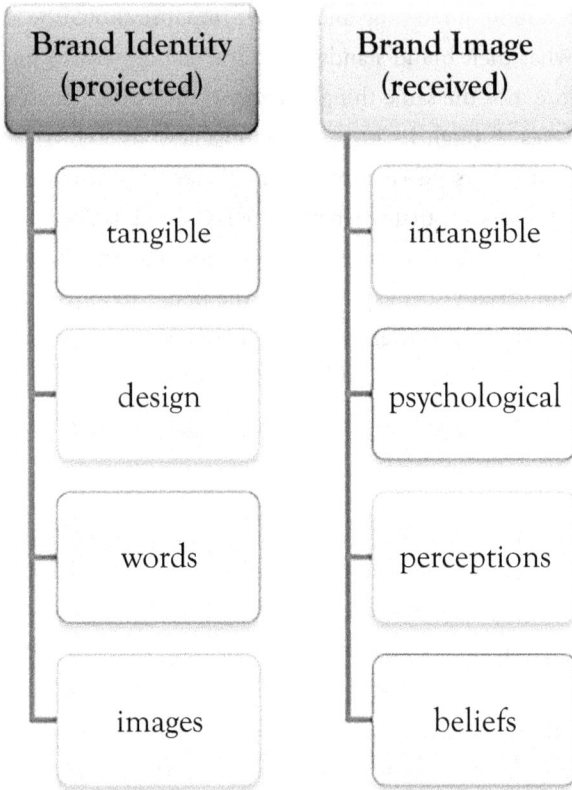

```
Brand Identity          Brand Image
  (projected)            (received)

    tangible              intangible

     design             psychological

     words               perceptions

     images                beliefs
```

Figure 2.2 Brand identity versus brand image—a comparison

As presented in Figure 2.2, brand imagery is, however, an entirely different creature. Whereas brand identity is a tangible, visual production that is projected, brand imagery is an intangible, psychological perception that is received. The brand owner can fully control how the brand identity is designed, manifested, and messaged in its communication by the company but can only at most hope to influence how the brand is perceived, understood, and valued in its reception by the customer.

> *Brand identity is a tangible, visual production that is projected;*
> *Brand imagery is an intangible, psychological perception*
> *that is received.*

This is because brand imagery is about the perception, psychology, and qualitative beliefs held by the customer and other stakeholders following their interaction, engagement, and experience with the brand in the market.

Brand imagery is a thing of the mind; it resides there as the residue of what has been experienced and believed about a brand's proposition, personality, and values. This image is of course shaped over time on the back of each individual encounter with the brand, be that via its consumption by the customer, its endorsement by one's peers, or its promotion by the company.

Brand image, therefore, is not fixed or set in stone but is malleable; it can be monitored and assessed, and this is the function of qualitative research and analysis; it can be influenced and changed, and this is the function of ongoing brand design and communications. So, a strong, outstanding, credible, and positive brand image (as opposed to identity) is the goal of every brand strategy, communications plan, and marketing program.

Branding Is Not a Science; It Is Not an Art; It Is a Process

Is branding a science or an art, I hear some folks ask! Well, I'm all for science and art, but essentially, it is the *process* of exploration and development that unearths and understands a brand's uniqueness, defines the brand strategy, and designs its visual expression and media communications. Science alone will not achieve this in that science denotes research and strategic think. Art alone will not achieve this, in that art majors on creative design and graphic communication. Process is by its nature more comprehensive, all-embracing, objective, and confident; it is more disciplined, structured, and methodical. It may prove to be more expensive and time-consuming to undertake, but also more rigorous, reliable, resilient and, therefore, confident in its outputs: its brand recommendations, creative solutions, and communication plans. This you can invest in!

75 Percent of What Makes a Brand Great Has Nothing to Do With the Product or Service Delivered!

Brands are not built just on product features or service components. They are not built merely on rational values (bigger, faster, cheaper …) or specifically on the functional product or service offer. They are built on experience, meaning the total experience that the consumer enjoys both at the functional and emotional level. It is this experience that constitutes the total value-add achieved by the consumer—the total enjoyment and value that the consumer gains from the product or service purchased. Most of this value gain can be attributed to personal identity and self-esteem benefits and how one feels and sees oneself in terms of personal affirmation, image, and/or association with peers. How a purchase makes us feel is more powerful than merely what a product does for us. So, what makes a brand great? Emotion—meaning the emotional bond achieved by a product or service in its purchase, use, and consumption over time. How one feels about a purchase, how one looks in using it, and how one is regarded by being associated with it are central to the lifetime experience and value achieved from a product or service. In short, emotional benefits have more—and more long-lasting—impact than functional benefits.

Of course, what the product or service does and how well it functions is fundamental: it must perform as advertised and be fit for purpose and up to the standard expected—meaning that it is essential that the product is effective and fully supports the consumer's bigger, emotional brand experience. But, that being achieved, there is so much more that a brand (as opposed to a product or service) can and does bring in terms of emotional reward and personal value. Do we buy a watch just to tell the time? Do we buy a car just to get from A to B? Do we wear clothes just to keep us warm? Do we buy a smartphone just to connect us to the world? Products become brands when they deliver much more than functional benefits; products become brands when they are conveyors of image, status, group identity, self-esteem. As Kapferer (2012) states in *The New Strategic Brand Management: Advanced Insights and Strategic Thinking,* "Products are mute: the brand gives them meaning and purpose, telling us how a product should be read. A brand is both a prism and a magnifying glass through which products can be decoded." Brands make people feel and look better; brands bond with consumers at the emotional level and build product–consumer relationships, which engender deep loyalty and preference, and deliver real value-for-money experiences.

Strong brands are emotional powerhouses that build and sustain market relationships over time and thereby increase the competitive advantage and commercial success of the brand owner. Brands are distinctive and powerful persuaders that strive constantly to understand and keep aligned with the consumer's mindset, desires, and deep-seated needs as these evolve. When a product or service achieves this relationship with its consumers, then it has become a brand and will have a reputation in the marketplace to prove it. As Kapferer continues, "Psychologists have also identified the halo effect as a major source of value created by a brand: the fact that knowing the name of the brand does influence consumer perception of the product advantages beyond what the visible cues had themselves indicated."

Whether we attribute 75, 70, 65, or 60 percent of a brand's greatness to nonproduct or service characteristics is not important *per se* and is, of course, grounds for healthy debate, but the point is that brands are built mostly on nontangible attributes that connect and are experienced by consumers at the emotional level. As such, brands are in a different commercial league than products and possess a very different perspective on their value proposition and purpose in the market and in people's lives and lifestyles.

The Brand Does Not Live in the Boardroom or the MD's Office. It Lives in the Marketplace

How often have we heard it said that a brand is a logo, or that a brand is a product, as if the words brand and logo are simply interchangeable or, likewise, that the words brand and product are interchangeable? Of course, if you're working in what I call a *brand university*—such as Unilever, Master Foods, Diageo, Proctor and Gamble—you will know exactly what a brand is, right? Because a brand is not a logo nor a product (no matter how good a product it is!) nor packaging nor something just sitting anonymously on a shelf in a supermarket! No, a brand is none of these things—a brand is essentially a relationship of relevant and unique added value for the customer. A brand is something that the customer understands (at least at an emotional level), identifies with and appreciates for its inherent value (including both functional and emotional values and points-of-difference). The brand's value will be defined and projected by the brand owner, but it is not until it is recognized, accepted, experienced, and enjoyed by the customer, and on a repeated basis (exhibiting trust!), that it can claim distinctiveness and loyalty in the market.

A brand is essentially a relationship of relevant and
unique added value for the customer.

My own definition of a brand, as cited elsewhere, is *uniqueness you know, want, and trust.* A brand is only a brand when it possesses uniqueness (or distinctive differential) in the market and has earned the trust of the customer or consumer. To have or to own a brand is to command the trust and loyalty of the consumer on an ongoing basis for the product or service proposition offered. Merely having a product does not qualify; merely having an attractive logo does not mean you have a relationship of trust and relevance with the consumer; merely having a product or a logo (or usually both) does not mean you have a brand. Your customer is the litmus test as to whether you have a brand or not: your customer will have an emotional relationship with your product or service and your logo because through these elements you communicate and deliver a sustainable consumption experience at a functional and emotional level (both are usually in play), which has stand-out and unique value-add in the market, and which, therefore, delivers demonstrable value for money. It is this creative chemistry between the brand and its consumer that gives life to the brand—and sales to its product—in the marketplace. The brand, therefore, not only grabs the attention of the customer but also builds and sustains a relationship of trust and relevance that engenders an emotional bond between the product and buyer. The fact is that *product* is actually superseded by the value-adding *proposition* that the brand is offering to the customer, and it is this proposition rather than merely the product (or service) alone that is understood by the customer, thus generating a sense of outstanding value and commanding strong customer loyalty in the user or consumption experience. This chemistry between brand and customer happens of course in the market and not back in the Boardroom or in the MD's office and, in this way, the brand unquestionably *lives* in the marketplace rather than in the company or at the point of production.

Brand Thinking Motivates an Organization and Magnifies Its Growth Potential. Without It, a Business Must Under-Exert, Under-Perform, and Under-Achieve

Do you work for a brand or work for a company? I mean it matters, doesn't it? It's a mindset, a way of thinking. Another way of expressing the point is: do you work for a brand or do you have a job? There is a difference, isn't there? I think it makes the world of difference to a person, to a company, and to the marketplace as to how employees think about what they do every day and who or what they are working for. The point is that pride in the job starts with pride in the brand, and pride in the brand is first and foremost within the employee domain. Okay, so you're asked by family, friends, fellow business folks "what do you do?"; answer: "I work for company xyz." Response: "Oh, what do they do?" Or, alternatively, some folks might answer: "I work for Google." Response: "Oh really. Wow! That's cool." Brand matters, which means brand name matters, which has all sorts of ramifications none more important than in the recruitment and retention of talent. So, even the mention of a company name can be a flat or an inspiring experience depending on whether the company is a well-known and well-liked brand or whether it is an anonymous, low-profile organization with little market recognition or brand resonance. Employee motivation, therefore, can start—or not— at the very mention of the company name for which they work, with the brand recognition and power of that company reflected in the immediate response of the questioner: ... Who do your work for? ... "Apple." "Hey, that's amazing!" or some such spontaneous expression of enthusiasm. And, of course, you don't have to work for a mega global brand to get such a positive reaction, but the brand has, of course, to be well known and admired in its own market territory.

Working for a brand is such a cool thing to do as long, of course, as that brand is in good stead in the market. During the 2008+ world recession, for example, it was not one bit cool to be a bank employee, and although most bank employees internationally had good job security, it was still extremely awkward for them to have to admit that they worked for a bank—particularly when that bank's reputation had been highly sullied, resulting in what could be called brand infamy! So, the brand of the organization you work for matters and is, of course, an immediate consideration when applying for a job. Is the employer a branded organization? What does its brand stand for? This matters in the world of employee recruitment and very much in the competitive and often onerous space of talent retention.

It also very much matters of course in determining the sustained morale and motivation levels of company employees—or at least in acting as an important contributory factor in employee motivation. As Mosley (2014) states in *Employer Brand Management: Practical Lessons from the World's Leading Employers*, "In the same way that leading companies strive to deliver uniquely valuable products and services, they also seek to shape a distinctive organizational culture and brand identity … . A strongly shared sense of culture and purpose can drive extraordinary levels of motivation, loyalty and performance … (A) powerful combination of differentiating capabilities and distinctive cultural identity helps to attract the 'right' kind of talent. It generates employee pride, advocacy and commitment."

Brand matters. Who I work for matters. Because what *they* stand for matters. And it matters at a rational level (who they are, what they do), it matters at an emotional level (they are well known and liked for their heritage, authentic values, and market prowess), and it matters at a personal level ("I really identify with this company, its values and vision, its personality, progressiveness and market position. It's really me!").

Whatever the reason is in each case, the company brand has the power to enthuse and motivate an organization, or not, as the case may be. "Hands-up who prefers to work for a high-profile, branded, highly-regarded organization with demonstrable values and a galvanizing vision?" Alternatively, "who prefers to work for an unknown, low-profile, commoditized organization with uncertain values and lacking expressed vision and personality?" Answers on a postcard please … (or just tweet!!).

But having a brand position in the marketplace that is widely recognized and highly regarded is possible only because of the strategic and dynamic brand thinking that underlies a confident communication of the brand's proposition. It is brand thinking that defines the rationale for a brand's uniqueness and competitive power and position. It is brand thinking, creatively expressed, that enthuses people, excites people, impassions people, and instigates people to embrace and champion the brand and the business.

Brand thinking and messaging is a tool around which people can and will become highly motivated given the right information, understanding, and enabling organizational development. In so doing, it beckons renewed management focus, strategic direction, and a time of change in which the growth of a company will be magnified. The rightful goal of brand thinking is to put people on a mission to change the world—somebody's world somewhere. Such a sense of mission inspires effort, entrepreneurship, ideas, performance, and achievement. Without the brand vision and its inherent thinking for positive change, innovation, even invention, the organization—the people employed—will under-exert and necessarily under-perform, at least relative to what is otherwise possible and achievable via brand-led thinking and brand-led transformation.

> *The rightful goal of brand thinking is to put people on a mission to change the world—somebody's world somewhere.*

In short, brand thinking should set the bar higher by visioning a future of new transformational experiences that bring unique, exciting added value to the target market and existing customer base. Anything less must underwhelm, under-deliver, and under-achieve, and in so doing, will under-impress and ultimately lead to demotivated employees. It is these very employees who are taking questions day and daily from all and sundry about who they work for, and what special value they and their company bring, and how that transforms lives and living for the good of people, society and the world ... or at least somebody's world somewhere.

There Are Three Levels of Brand Creation: New Brands, Refreshed Brands, Rebrands

I think this needs said: not all branding programs are either about the original design of new brands or the complete rebranding of old ones! Too often, folks, when they hear the word *brand*, think "brand change = expensive total overhaul of our entire business!" Wrong. More often than not, brand work is in the space of refreshing, revitalizing, evolving; therefore, evolution not revolution! In fact, a *total rebrand* (from an existing proposition to a new proposition) is a rare enough creature to find in our digitized communications jungle. Let's think for a moment about the real intent of this language—therefore what the full reach and meaning of a *rebrand* is. Remember that a brand strategy is like a bridge between the corporate vision and the customer experience (a toll bridge actually because you of course pay for the pleasure!). The brand strategy recognizes that to bring an exciting cutting-edge new brand proposition to market, it must encompass, engage, and coordinate all stakeholders and audiences both inside and outside the organization. No mean feat! This takes time and money (usually much more time than money), requiring a deft touch, inclusive communications planning, and thorough execution across diverse and often (but of course by no means always) large employee bases. Rebranding is an internal organizational exercise as much as it is an external marketing one, and as such, it has to have depth as well as breadth. Rebranding, by its nature, is indeed all-encompassing, sweeping all before it as the transition from old to new, from yesterday to tomorrow, from *know-you* to *new-you* takes the brand to the market highways and byways to gain and sustain market traction and brand market share. A rebrand, by its nature, leaves no corners untouched and no stones unturned in transitioning to the future, and doing so is indeed major marketing surgery and definitely not just a mere identity face-lift! Rebrands, therefore, are neither commonly needed nor commonplace. Most companies don't need them or do them—or rarely, if ever. They are the marketing exception rather than the rule.

The other knee-jerk thought process often involves regarding brand change as meaning simply the design of a new logo. Wrong again! At the very least, a *new logo* means that the organization is committing to a new visual identity for all its visual marketing collateral and its internal employee and cross-company or group communications. This necessitates the immediate redesign of all that the brand identity touches—everything from corporate stationery to product packaging, to website and digital communications, advertising and promotional materials, all marketing literature, point of sale, videography, and so on … , meaning it must be no-holds-barred in applying the new logo into a reconfigured brand identity for the organization. This demands an overhaul of the entire brand identity system of the organization and also reproduction and dissemination of detailed supporting brand identity guidelines.

This, of course, notwithstanding the preparation of new design guidelines, does not constitute a *new brand*; it simply constitutes a new logo (or identity). No, a new brand is something completely different in intent, objective, and scope. A new brand does not currently exist or have presence in the market. A new brand, whether it be for an existing company or a new start-up, whether it be a corporate-level brand or a product-level brand, will not be achieved by a mere logo design project. A new brand for a company—small, medium, or large—necessitates the definition of a brand strategy that takes rigorous account of the corporate purpose, the customer need, and the competitive opportunity in the market. It also, critically, must take into account the unique style, personality, tone of voice, values, emotional connection, and brand proposition that the new brand will position itself on for enduring relevance and competitive appeal in the market. Like a rebrand process, the work to create a new brand is large in scope, ambitious in reach, thorough in analysis, and innovative in creativity. Or, at least it should be! The more distance that a new brand can put between itself and its competitive set, the more probability of course that market traction and commercial success will follow. The braver the brand the better—but always based on real customer insights and distinctive creativity and messaging. Stand-out is everything for brands and particularly so for new-to-market brands. So, a new brand deserves and needs *the works* in terms of market insight, thought leadership, brand definition, and creative expression if it's to be fit for purpose (and stand a chance!) in the market; an existing brand does not. An existing brand already has an established presence, legacy, and heritage in the market—it has a known and recognized back-story. An existing brand typically needs what I would call a brand refresh—a reinvigoration of the existing brand offer and its visual communications in order to reposition it for enhanced relevance and value perception in its served target market.

> *Stand-out is everything for brands and particularly so*
> *for new-to-market brands.*

A brand refresh, therefore, is about evolution not revolution but being so does not mean that it should be treated lightly or left hanging in the pending tray indefinitely! Be clear, a brand refresh is a major statement by the organization that its market proposition is on the march, that its underlying value offer has been reconfigured, and that the future of the brand and its relationship with the customer and the marketplace has been reviewed, reconsidered, reprioritized, and recommunicated. This is tender loving care (TLC) for the brand and what it stands for, how it expresses itself and its innate value and experience delivery in the market. A *refresh*, however, still means wholesale (but not total) change, in that it reflects a modernization of thinking, positioning, and strategic intent, all reflected of course through an evolved design and identity visualization. Postlaunch, customers should immediately identify with the refreshed brand and recognize it as a definite enhancement of the existing brand offer and its relevance for them. A successful brand refresh will let the customer (and the distribution channels) know that the brand owner/manufacturer/supplier understands and cares about their needs; it will demonstrate care and dedication to the company–customer business relationship, and that the brand owner is actively investing in the brand's future strength, growth, and longevity in the market. A brand refresh is, therefore, not only a redesign of the brand identity but is a sign of commitment, creativity, and confidence and indeed of the professionalism of the organization in caring for its customers and earning their ongoing loyalty—and not taking this for granted. In my experience, the vast majority of brand projects are *brand refreshes* rather than new brand creations or merely logo redesigns, and certainly not entire rebrands.

Planning Branding

Don't Think Branding First. Think Brand Proposition

Too many people default to *the logo* when they first think about a brand. It's the lowest denomination of thought when in fact the proposition of the brand, which is so often the proposition of the business itself, should be the first thought. Ask yourself "what do we stand for? What is our proposition to the world?" before you go to "do we need a new logo?" Amazingly, frustratingly, too often, the first thought is the small play rather than the big idea. Now… why are we in business? What do we do that is great… unique even?

Brand Strategy Is Not About Getting It Perfect. It's About Getting It Together

Will your brand values model and strategic thinking be perfect? Probably not, but it doesn't need to be. A half a loaf is better than no bread, and a quantum leap in brand thinking trumps no fresh thinking whatsoever. Don't look for perfection, even precision, rather look for cohesion, joined-up thinking. For example, strive for initial alignment among the directors or leadership team about what the brand stands for today and what its potential is for the future—then work to grow this into a consensus and expand your brand understanding over time; seek agreement on your core brand values and brand essence and on the functional and emotional experience your customer is to get; craft up your brand proposition working in close collaboration with your fellow directors and decision makers; have ongoing discussions about the brand's competitive position, points of difference, and target market; explore and evaluate branding strategies and your design and communication practice. Believe me, things are going to be different and innovative for your business from here forward. Just get going and get it together!

Be Patient. Constructing a Brand Model Takes a Number of Iterations

To be honest, it is not often in a typical company's experience that the *brand model* is put on the table for creation, discussion, or evolution. Too often, it can be tarnished with the *mission, vision, corporate statement* brush, and the whole endeavor can seem tiresome and time-consuming in advance. The surprise and irony are that, when time is eventually allocated, the experience is exciting, and the process highly engaging and motivating. Or, it can and should be! And, of course, it's not meant to be easy or simple in execution. But it is so worth it. And naturally, it will not be cracked on the first outing. That's not how business works. The process is and has got to be iterative, taking a series of attempts, a number of steps, and always involving the leadership team. So be patient, involve the right players, keep momentum in the process, and believe in the outcome.

Research till You Can Predict the Next Response

One of the discoveries about research is that you don't have to research everybody and you don't have to research forever. More is not necessarily better. Research is an insight and confidence-producing process, with confidence growing with every interview, with every survey, and usually quickly so when you're talking to the right target audience. There comes a point in every research project, therefore, where you believe you have the information, insight, and confidence that you have achieved your research goal: you have reached the heart of the research matter, you have made a key finding, discovered an illuminating insight, you feel you can even predict the next interviewee's response. This is the point of maximum return on research time and investment. To cease the process any earlier than this makes for a less confident result; to extend the process any longer than this makes for a comparative waste of valuable time and resources. The trick is to have the clarity and confidence to decide when you have achieved your research goal.

Qualitative Research Is Essential to Brand Understanding

In the world of branding, perception is reality, emotion is energy, personality is power and, therefore, *qualitative* (*how it makes me feel*) research is invaluable, vital, essential. The point is that brands thrive on emotion because we human beings are emotional creatures. Of course, *quantitative* factors (*what it is/does*) are relevant and sometimes crucial, but they are in themselves a minimalist way of regarding or approaching the building of brands. They are only at most a starting point and are generally insufficient to sustain brand appeal, loyalty, and innovation.

> *In the world of branding, perception is reality, emotion is energy, personality is power.*

In extolling the virtues and suitability of qualitative over quantitative research for brands, *Developing Brands with Qualitative Market Research* (Owen 2002) explains that "Fluidity and responsiveness are key aspects of the qualitative approach. Here there is a clear contrast with the more fixed character of quantitative research which poses precisely structured questions to generate a more numeric result; that is, straightforward 'question and answer' research." And to rationalize why such a *fluidity of research* approach is key, the author emphasizes that "In the ideal qualitative work, what structure there is, is designed to help things emerge. The ideal is that structure should never be applied too rigidly as this will inhibit or constrain what comes out." This, in a word, is the fundamental flaw in resorting primarily to quantitative methods when researching the emotionally charged and experiential world of brands. So, why confine yourself to a focus on quantitative characteristics when defining, designing, and communicating a brand proposition? That makes no sense at all when there are oodles of emotional and personality possibilities and values to bolt onto and into the brand-building strategy.

So, make sure to prioritize qualitative research to probe deeply the emotional values and needs of your customers—the findings of which will form the basis of your future brand proposition. For brands, quantitative is merely the starting gate; qualitative is where the real action and depth is and where the true potential and strength of the company, product, and brand power resides and routes out off. To think big in branding is to search for and understand the emotional components of the brand experience. Qualitative research and insights power this thinking and drive so much of a brand's distinctiveness, market value, and unique consumer appeal.

Make Personality the Rich Relation

Personality is everything in branding—or almost everything—but its role and application are generally misunderstood to such a degree that it can be treated as somewhat the *poor relation* of brand development. Next to the rational/functional values and emotional values, personality attributes are defined to specify the nature of the behavior of a brand, its style of expression, its tone of voice. This specifies how a brand is to communicate—what its personality is to be—that will, on the one hand, be consistent with the underlying brand strategy, values, and proposition and, on the other, be in tune with key target audience requirements and expectations of style and tone. In short, personality ensures that the brand is communicated with a style and tone that is most acceptable and relevant to the target market.

Personality is, therefore, powerful karma in brand communications and will determine how the words and imagery of the brand design and creative expression work-phase will be crafted, selected, and visually applied. The brand's personality will of course be expressed in both visual and nonvisual media platforms, from corporate identity to packaging to website to video production to print advertising to TV, radio, digital marketing, and social media messaging. It should communicate as one, singular, confident, self-aware, and self-assured personality, be that youthful or mature, male or female, urban or rural, wise or wacky, Irish or Italian, foodie or vegan, gentleman or vagabond, energetic or sedentary, sporty or sagacious, savvy or salacious. And it must do so immediately whether that be in the world of food, science, government, media, digital, transport, manufacturing, electronics, pharma, or biotech. Wherever it be positioned, and to whatever audience, the brand will be tasked with communicating the product plus the proposition plus the personality of the value offer to the market. It must do so in a confident and consistent manner where the style and personality of its behavior and communication will be a brand signature of some power and recognition.

Creating Branding

Make Sure the Creative Gets the Big Idea, Not Just the Written Brief

Writing a great creative brief is an art in itself and is vital to a professional approach to branding development. Rightly, therefore, there is a lot of time and attention paid to this discipline by professional design and marketing institutes internationally. Nevertheless, the sad fact of life is that many design and communications projects proceed without an adequate brief on the basis that devolving responsibility for creative ideas to the designer or communications creative will suffice. It won't. When considering the whole panorama of varying company sizes, formal design or communications briefs can be few and far between; if focusing on larger organizations then, yes, creative briefs will be notably much more in evidence, but even here, the quality will vary enormously and too often the essential underlying creative direction or *big idea* can be missing in whole or in part from the briefing document.

Even where creative briefs are formally developed and structured, they can often major on background business and brand information, waxing lyrical about historical brand evolution, branding development to date, key markets, target segments, market trend data, business resourcing, structuring, and company ownership changes afoot or imminent in the future. Too frequently, the creative brief can dance around the issue of what should be at the heart of a creative or design brief: a unique and differentiating creative idea. It is one thing to write and organize a creative brief, it is another to invest it with innovative value and meaningful creative direction. The crucial thing is that the creative brief is the essential bridge between the brand strategy and its creative interpretation and visual expression; it must explicitly direct the creative team and confidently focus their work in design, copywriting, digital and broader communications. A great creative brief of course achieves this, and yet, a great creative brief on its own is not enough to guarantee an authentic and faithful brand expression, communication, or creative delivery.

The problem is that a miscommunication can occur whenever the written brief meets the creative hand, or when left-brain thinking and direction (the written brief) meets right-brain perspective and interpretation (the creative resource). Often I wonder if the creative reads the briefing document closely enough—and sometimes if they even read it at all! I remember once famously winning a competitive pitch in the public sector where one of the contenders had presented a proposed creative solution that was no match for the brand needs as they were eventually defined and agreed by the client. Here was a case of a senior designer jumping-the-gun because he believed he knew best from his considerable experience what the client and the brand needed! He didn't. And such creative arrogance in defiance of professional and robust briefing ignores new ideas, pays scant regard to fresh innovation, and devalues the entire creative process. To do so is to jeopardize the expression and implementation of brand innovation; it portrays a cynicism toward the underlying strategic planning, market insights, and business case behind the creative initiative; it underestimates the potential for achieving a truly unique, visionary, and competitive differentiation and positioning in the market.

In larger organizations, marketing directors and brand managers are tasked with overseeing and supervising the briefing process; in smaller organizations, it will be the owners or their general managers who take on this vital responsibility. The key of course is that, even when the written brief is cohesive, comprehensive, and sufficiently creative in direction, the relationship between the briefing executive and the commissioned creative must be one of openness, understanding, partnership, and trust. The written creative brief and the briefing process represent a moment of intense focus and client–creative interaction in which much is at stake in the transference of brand strategy insights and intent into the creative realm. This handover of one distinct skillset (strategic) to another (creative) initiates the process of visual and design expression and brand creation that must ultimately leave its mark not merely on graphics or packaging or communications but in the marketplace, and therefore on the mind of the customer and eventual consumer. To achieve this, the creative needs to *get* the brief in more ways than one and deeply so; receiving the written brief is not enough, no matter how professionally written and comprehensive it proves to be; it must be personally and inspiringly presented by its author; it must then be carefully read, deeply understood, and creatively embraced in order to maximize the brand's expression, experience, and effective engagement in the market.

Aim for a Strong Identity. Be Brave With Colors and Imagery

The enemy of great branding is visual mimicry, and the perfect way to counter this is to be brave with colors and imagery. So often in business sectors, companies will look around at their corporate peers as if for acceptance, and feel reassured that they conform to the general look and feel of their sector, that they fit in with other sectoral players, and that they can't be accused of stepping out of the accepted identity norm or presenting any differently than leading competitors. The syndrome is one of "we look as good as the rest, and that'll do fine." But that's the problem, it'll not do fine; it doesn't do to strive for sameness, to seek to just fit in, or to be just as good as everyone else in your sector. That's not branding, that's conforming, and it's surprisingly commonplace among established businesses. Think, for example, of well-known businesses in the financial services industry, they love to emphasize the color blue in their identities (Allianz, Deutsche Bank, Visa, Zurich, PayPal, …) as do many of the major car brands (VW, Ford, GM, Mazda, Hyundai, …) and online businesses (LinkedIn, Facebook, Twitter, Skype, …).

While the psychology of color (blue confers trustworthy, conservative, safe, reliable, even masculine) is of course an important consideration in identity color choice, for the sake of brand distinction and visual differentiation, it is crucial to design the brand identity for visual stand-out. By definition, this means being distinctive by presenting differently from other market players and competitors. But to do so takes a level of courage in decision making around the creative process and an understanding and confidence in just how far to take visual differentiation. Depending on the market sector in question, getting the balance right may mean achieving at least a visual differentiation from existing color and design norms in the market; alternatively, it may mean *breaking the mold* and setting a whole new benchmark for communication and use of color in the face of an otherwise predictable and staid world of sectoral branding.

Likewise, use of imagery is also a great potential driver of differentiation, and so, it is vital to stay away from standard and overused stock images of, for example, globes and handshakes and briefcases and airplanes and lightbulbs and the like. You know them, we've all seen them, they're everywhere. And that's the point, they are everywhere, they're hackneyed, and they demonstrate a lack of creativity and uniqueness, and even a basic lack of care and attention in planning and expressing your brand identity and communications. Be brave with color and with imagery and definitely be different; do not fit in with the brand-set in your sector, but be courageous for the sake of demonstrating creativity and the distinctiveness of your brand. If you have to compromise on color, do so with courage: be colorful rather than colorless; be bright rather than boring; be so youthful rather than so yesterday; and as much as possible, be energetic and exciting. Do not be the same as others—branding is all about visual stand-out, and about matching that with a differential, energizing customer experience.

Believe in the Power of Poetry in Business. Words Can Sing

I've been writing business documents for many years: discussion documents; proposals; reports; slide presentations ... and was well coached in my early days in PA Consulting Group on how to plan, structure, and proof a client document. The standard was high, joined-up thinking and sequencing was a must; spelling mistakes were not tolerated. PA definitely gave me a real *tool* for taking with me into my brand consulting career, so

I knew early in life what a great standard of proposal and report looked like, and I've successfully used this learning as the basis for written documents ever since. Structure, sequencing, and spellings are one thing, but word choice and use of words are quite another. This was something I became aware of later on in developing my own written style. I call it *poetry in business.*

There is a certain legality of content and tone that is usually expected and necessary in a formal commercial document—and certainly in proposal documents—and yet, around that, there is so much more scope to embellish business documents over and above the minimal requirement of specifying a methodology or detailing research findings or strategy recommendations. This is what I mean by the use of poetry in business: I am referring specifically to the written word and how a document often needs to speak for itself when received by the client or distributed standalone among the management team or executive decision makers. The document in these circumstances needs indeed to speak up for itself, and the better it does that, the more effective it will be in persuading management about its objectives, recommendations, and investment value. A happy hobby-horse of mine here is alliteration. I believe in it, I practise it, I love it. Alliteration is defined as: "The occurrence of the same letter or sound at the beginning of adjacent or closely connected words" (Oxford English Dictionary). Of course, overuse is never ever a good thing, but to pepper a paper with poetic pronouncements can be perceived as positively professional! Well, you know what I mean!! I believe in the power of the poetic in human communication, and business and brands are no less responsive to the trick. Effective use of alliteration also highlights the potential for words to do more than merely inform but to inspire, more than merely talk but to sing. Words that talk inform; words that sing inspire.

Words that talk inform; words that sing inspire.

Clearly, apart from alliteration, there is the basic choice of words that form the content of the document. A varied use of vocabulary is essential to a professional document in order to guard against, among other things, the overuse of specific words in the same or proximate sentences. Any such repetition can throw the impact of the message by demonstrating an apparent lack of care and attention to the construction or phrasing of a sentence or paragraph. Word switching is key to delivering a statement or message in a professional manner. A classic example of the role of word switching in text is the use and repetition of the word to describe the people employed in the company or organization: for example, do you call them employees, staff, management, colleagues, human resources, talent, teams, or simply people? The choice of the word is important to get right within the context of the company type, its culture, and tone of voice, and for the type of document being created. In using *staff* in one sentence, do you repeat that same word in the next sentence/s or switch to *employees*? If emphasizing *colleagues* in one paragraph, do you switch in the next paragraph to *people*? Experience teaches that overuse is the enemy of how a document reads; it is best to go for a variation in word choice that, while it may be unnecessary at a purely logical and informational level, does result in a better sounding document. Word variation makes for a better and more convincing read. It suggests the document has been more carefully considered in its preparation, and it sounds more professional, literate, and indeed intelligent in its thinking. This is all to the good of the document's power of persuasion, which is, of course, its precise purpose as a piece of business communication (… or is that business *prose*?!).

Purposefully expressing things in multiples, and particularly in groups of three, also adds distinctly to the sound of a document—to the lilt of how it reads. Again, careful construction of words in threesomes will reflect that due attention, thought, and consideration has been given to the creation of the idea and the construction of the document. This duly conveys a sense of depth of idea, quality of thinking, and importance of the message, including the brand message. Of course, the power of multiples is that it extends, qualifies, and re-emphasizes the key import of an idea and deepens the reader's understanding accordingly. And, indeed, you needn't stick to *threes*, you can stretch the repetition further, but this requires that you have a good ear for how the sentence sounds, its aural balance, and its limitations in terms of length and wordiness. To emphasize the point, here are some examples of alliteration and three-word constructions that I've used in this chapter on *Secrets and Lessons from the Leading Edge*:

Examples showing three-word constructions:

> *"There comes a point in every research project where you believe that you have the information, the insight and the confidence"*
>
> *"They are only a starting point and are generally insufficient to sustain brand appeal, loyalty and innovation"*
>
> *"So why stop with quantitative characteristics when defining, designing and communicating a brand proposition"*
>
> *"Qualitative insights power this thinking and drive so much of a brand's distinctiveness, market value and consumer appeal"*
>
> *"Celebration is the secret weapon—this will help people 'to become motivated' by recognising their talents, their efforts, their achievements"*
>
> *"The project leadership needs to engage with these important influencers and listen for and to their sincerely and strongly held opinions, aspirations and expectations"*
>
> *"Brand performance, effectiveness and success depends on people inculcating it at an emotional level"*
>
> *"A 'living the brand' approach, standard and programme is vital to engendering and sustaining a deep and meaningful and transformative brand culture and holistic corporate experience"*
>
> *"Such a revelation signals an opportunity to get close to the client executive and become involved in thought leadership, idea generation and expert participation in the briefing process"*
>
> *"Very often, the client executive responsible for preparing the project brief will appreciate a second-opinion, a sounding-board or indeed a convenient helping-hand in developing, validating and finalising a comprehensive, well-thought-through and robust project brief"*

Examples showing three-word constructions in alliterative form:

> *"Structure, sequencing and spellings are one thing but word choice and use-of-words are quite another"*
>
> *"Having worked on branding and brand development assignments for almost three decades, here are some of my discoveries, definitions and descriptions"*
>
> *"It may therefore be more expensive and time-consuming to undertake, but also more rigorous, reliable, resilient and, therefore, confident in its outputs"*

"A brand's identity is the universal visual expression of the brand to any-one, anywhere, anyhow"

"But the creative and business challenge comes in how to correlate, coordi-nate and communicate words and images"

"A brand refresh is, therefore, not only a redesign of the brand identity but is a sign of commitment, creativity and confidence"

"It's empirical, inspirational and even emotional stuff and requires having your best branding brains at the table to challenge, cajole and create the next big idea"

"This takes energy, enthusiasm and efficiency without which a brand campaign must be destined to flounder or even to fail. Fruitful outcomes depend on passion and persistence (and of course a great product) and such internal cross-company commitment must be recognised and rewarded"

And of course, all attempts at a little actual poetry or poetical approach, rare as these may be, never go amiss and do spice up a business or brand document, adding to the weight and import of the final written piece. Here's two examples drawn from this chapter:

"On such competences and disciplines are market changes read, alterna-tive plans displayed and brand decisions made"

"Where verbosity was vanity, now brevity was beauty and was valued as such by more modern communications practitioners"

Create the Name and Take the Credit

As the tongue-in-cheek saying goes … "what's in a name?" Well, the point is there's more than we realize of course. I have found that the naming of a new brand is of compelling interest to all brand watchers, and not just the brand owners but all audiences in the relevant sector, be they customers, prospects, or indeed neither. "Did you create the name?" I hear them ask as if name creation was the most skilled of all the brand development activities and as if naming is what really proves the brand consultant's worth! To say *yes* is to be instantly bestowed by the ques-tioner with the full credit for the entire brand development program, with the expectation that the name-generator has been responsible for all aspects of the brand's creation. I have found that the inverse also holds: that to answer *no* to the question leaves the respondent despondent! This is because even though you may have otherwise planned and led the entire development and creative and design execution processes, you will nonetheless be regarded as being devoid of all responsibility and executive function in bringing the new brand to life—all because the brand naming was done (indeed often merely just completed!) by the client themselves.

People like to know who created the name; they are less interested or impressed by who designed the logo, who wrote the tagline, who produced the video, who shot the photography, who created the website, who planned the brand strategy, never mind who ran the research or whose original idea it was in the first place that inspired the brand's creation! No, none of this matters as much, if at all, in comparison with the name!: "who created the name?" That's what ultimately bestows proof of brand talent, that's what sorts the innovators from the imitators, that's what proves your marketing metal, that's what matters to the onlooker!

In the world of branding, we know very well that *perception is reality*, and so it is; so go on and throw your hands up in the air as you might … the masses will simply ask "did you create the name?," so tell them yeah or nay, to your instant credit or discredit as the case may be: "you mean you did everything except create the name? Okay, but tell us then *who* created the name?!" To create the brand name is to take the creative credit. And that's fine with me, as long as it's no one else but the client!

Briefing Branding

Clients Do Not Buy What They Do Not Like. Take Regular Soundings on Identity Design Expectations and Preferences

Demonstrating the professional process is vital and powerful in convincing clients that your visual identity shortlist and recommendations are worthy, warranted, and well-thought-through, as well as being substantiated by relevant research soundings and even market testing. Even so, a robust process and empirical research are still not enough to persuade management decision makers that your shortlisted visual identities contain a winning, never mind outstanding, creative direction. The client team may be with you all the way through the early design development stages, usefully feeding in practical observations, intelligent questions and creative suggestions en route, but as the process advances, and in particular when it reaches its final decision-making stage, then a different, cooler eye is often cast upon the proceedings and discussions by the client executives, namely, from the point of view of "do I like it?" Even when—as it should have been—any such objection was identified and prehandled throughout the course of the project, there is always room and opportunity, under the pressure of reaching a final choice, to shy off making a decision even when the evidence, rationale, and selection criteria are all well satisfied. The process may be complete (or almost) and the logic for the selection clearly laid out, and yet the client or client team still does not endorse the recommendation. Why? Because although they see the logic, sense, and rationale underpinning the identity recommendation, they have not engaged emotionally with the final creative output, leaving them as yet uncertain and unconvinced. In short, the client does not like the solution and therefore will not, and cannot, approve it. It may well be that they cannot even explain why they don't like the identity proposed, but, to their frustration and the frustration of all parties, it just *doesn't feel right* with the result that they cannot get behind it and won't back it in front of the broader management and employee team.

We want the client to like the work—the outcome of the work; we want the client to be excited, even passionate about it; and to be confident about recommending it to direct colleagues and employees throughout the company. A design solution presentation on its own will not normally guarantee this outcome, and it is, therefore, essential to take regular soundings on identity design expectations and preferences throughout the course of the work, including from the very earliest conceptual stages of graphic development. Ideally, at the end of the process, there should be no surprise lack of support or unforeseen questions or unexpected challenges to the design directions shortlisted for recommendation, and yet, it is so often the case that the presentation of the final candidate design solutions is marked by much uncertainty and anxiety. Clearly, the more emotional the engagement that is achieved with client decision makers throughout the creative development process, the greater the confidence in the presentation of final shortlisted designs. Ultimately, clients want to and need to like the final graphic solution if they are to feel capable of embracing the visual change and championing the new identity companywide and in the market. *Liking it* may not at the outset be seen as a priority process goal, nor indeed does it sound very professional, but in reality, it is a real boon to have management liking and even loving the new visual direction. In this eventuality, you will certainly sense their excitement, enthusiasm, and appetite for recommending the identity development to their respective direct reports, teams, employees, and peers. This result constitutes a successful project outcome, and also in due course, an impressive client testimonial for the creative consulting team and, similarly, valuable prospect referrals further down the line.

Clients Do Not Buy What They Do Not Understand. Explain the Brand Principles, Psychology, and Practicality for All Identity Design Components

While previously I have emphasized the ultimate importance of clients *liking* new identity design options or recommendations, it is also critical that clients understand the underlying principles of the branding brief and brand development goal on which the entire creative initiative is founded. If clients—or client team representatives—do not sufficiently understand the brand project or its rationale, then they will not buy it— meaning they will not feel equipped to endorse its visual recommendations nor invest in its implementation.

Brand identity components typically will include color, typography, and iconography, and sometimes, will include a new name. To make a reasoned, informed, and confident judgment on presented visual identity options or recommendations, the client (or executive team) must be introduced to, or updated on, the underlying strategy behind the brand that is presently subject to design development. Branding—the visual interpretation and expression of the brand's innate idea and uniqueness—must adhere to, and deliver on, the strategy behind the brand: its values (functional and emotional), its personality attributes (how it is to behave), its essential proposition (what it believes of itself and promises to the customer). Identity design components must serve the brand proposition and values by visually signaling and expressing the uniqueness of the brand's offer and experience promise.

In this sense, the brand identity must be designed to encapsulate and reference the principles of the brand: its nature and unique added value; the psychology of the brand: its personality, attitude, and mindset; and the practicalities of the brand: its colors, shapes, and sizing. In short, it is paramount that the brand identity is designed to be suitable for utilization and replication across a whole universe of diverse marketing applications and media. Colors, shapes, iconography, typography must all be chosen and crafted to create a brandmark and identity that are faithful to the brand's inherent proposition and strategy, and that is consistent with the experience, personality, and values that the brand is to become known for. Demonstrating and explaining how this is achieved is a vital necessity in ensuring an effective approval and efficient completion of the identity design phase of any branding or rebranding project. Designers and design directors must check for such understanding en route, from the project get-go.

Do Not Patronize Clients. Encourage "The Stupid Question." They Will Need to Understand the Design Strategy, Visual Options, and Recommended Solution Rationale

Most clients are not brand experts, and so, often, are unfamiliar (at the outset anyway) with the language of brand strategy or branding. They are, however, committed to the brand project, meaning that they are brand believers who know that the *brand* for them is a competitive opportunity, even necessity, if their business is to reach its rightful competitive position and full commercial potential in the market. Clients are intuitive, savvy, and can possess a deep passion for brand development, even though they might previously be inexperienced in investing in substantial, transformational brand change. While such enthusiasm and commitment to the project are always energizing, branders and creatives must not simply assume that the client facing them is well versed in the process of brand creation or familiar with the techniques or tactics of design development. To treat the client from the outset as if they should already understand the basics of design strategy and practice is to patronize, and doing so fails to bring the client effectively along the journey of understanding, creative inputting, and executive decision making that is essential to achieving the best project outcome. I am a believer in always encouraging *the stupid question* and in creating a positive environment of partnership and trust with the client team in which an open relationship can be fostered and leveraged. It is in this climate of openness and trust that deep understanding will be achieved with respect to the design strategy, rationale, visual options, and recommended solutions that design offers. This open way of working also brings confidence in the process employed and dependability on the buy-in sought and obtained from the client throughout the creative journey. Ensuring easy, open designer–client communication is a must if design solution options are to be thoroughly understood, properly evaluated, and a final solution confidently selected and enthusiastically approved.

Anticipate and Keep Ahead of Inevitable Client Queries. Beat Them to the E-Mail or the Phone Call

This may seem obvious, but in reality, it is an art form in itself. Think of the amount of selling time and effort that is invested in customer relationship development in advance of the sale, with fastidious care taken to follow up a prospect's expression of interest for a meeting, to seek updates on their internal discussions and ultimately feedback on proposals presented. Attention to detail, well-timed communications, and meticulous relationship management are the name of the game. And then, the sale closes, and the impetus of communications shifts with the switching of hats: the internal buyer becomes the internal manager; the selling consultant becomes the operating consultant (at least in the case of the smaller agencies or independent practitioners). The danger here is that the attention to communications, which prevailed during the selling process, becomes diluted, as consulting priorities shift to project activity and operations management. This can lead to a slacking in the timing or frequency of client contact for the purposes of progress updates, project discussions, and performance feedback. In such a scenario, the temptation can be to reduce client communications and *just get on with the work* and especially if the client manager is not particularly active in seeking updates or apparently disinterested in closely monitoring the detail of weekly project progress. Don't be fooled, the call will come! While postproject launch, the responsibility to monitor and keep in touch with project progress is a heightened obligation for the client, he may not always exercise that duty with the required regularity that could be expected. In such circumstances, where the operating consultant or consulting team are working hard on the job in hand, prudence must prevail. The client enquiry is sure to come, even if belatedly and, in anticipation of this, it is always smart to keep ahead of the client query by beating them to the e-mail, phone call, or text. By doing so, the consultant has, so to speak, the moral upper hand in conveying any surprising, awkward, or difficult news about project progress because he, not the client, has taken the initiative to make the call. And even where the contact is merely to update on regular progress, the initiative coming from the managing or operating consultant demonstrates care, transparency, and professionalism. In my experience, making the early or timely call helps greatly in diffusing any potential issues. It avoids or minimizes the growth of any anxieties that otherwise the client may experience relating to progress against schedule, team interaction, administration issues, research findings, or planned or interim outcomes. Clients are universally thankful for receiving timely updates, rather than having to regularly seek or chase these, and the sense of the consulting relationship is reinforced as one of easy access, openness, transparency, and trust. Knowing when to *make that call* demonstrates good understanding of the client, good attention to the project, and good time management, as well as, of course, adept customer relationship skills.

Pitching for Work? Inform the Brief to Transform Your Chance

Pitching for work is such a trial—particularly public sector pitching. It consumes huge amounts of resource, including on creative development, and it costs, costs, costs! By contrast, proposing for work—meaning in the private sector or for below-budget-ceiling projects—is of course by no means so harrowing, but you certainly want to have your creative wits about you and everything playing in your favor to see off experienced and innovative creative competition. Even with a good track record in winning your fair share of pitches and proposals, nothing is ever certain, definitely not a sure thing, and, in this business development endeavor, a modicum of good luck doesn't ever go amiss! Maximizing one's chances is of course the name of the game, and one way to transform your chance is to inform the brief. This is usually down to timing: that the timing of your prospection visit aligns adroitly with the development of the project brief.

The scenario is that a large private or public sector organization will usually be considering or preparing a written brief, and a well-timed prospection visit with the relevant executive will identify that the project is in planning, or that the briefing document is under consideration or is, in fact, actually at hand. Such a revelation signals an opportunity to get close to the client executive and become involved in thought leadership, idea generation, and expert participation in the briefing process. Very often, the client executive responsible for preparing the project brief will appreciate a second opinion, a sounding board, or indeed, a convenient helping hand. This can work to greatly assist and reassure the client in developing, validating, and finalizing a comprehensive, well-thought-through, and robust project brief—be that for a brand, creative, communications, or broader marketing scope of works. Participation in this thinking and preparation stage naturally positions the consultant with an excellent opportunity to then pitch for the work with a greater level of confidence. The client executive will, of course, be glad of the contribution made on shaping the goals, priorities, scope, and process of the project, and the supporting consultant or agency will naturally be well-positioned to submit a highly relevant proposal that fits well with their in-house approach, proprietary methodologies, resource capacity, and unique or differential skillsets. In this way, to inform the brief is to transform your chance of winning the project. Where this is for a company in the private sector, the impact is not only favorable but formidably so; where this is for an organization in the public sector, this effect will, of course, be diminished due to the specific strictures and evaluation criteria applying in relation to the acquisition and assessment of tender submissions. Nonetheless, in any case, to inform the brief is to tangibly improve and even transform the chance of success, and nowhere more evident is this than with all those prospect organizations that work free of tender process restrictions to make autonomous decisions about their preferred supplier. In such cases, with an established relationship, idea sharing, and collaborative working already in place, informing the brief does indeed transform the chance of winning the business, whether that requires contesting a competitive pitch process or not.

Implementing Branding

Under-Promise and Over-Deliver. It's an Age-Old Principle That Has Stood the Test of Time—A Real Smart Strategy in the Fast-Moving World of a Branding Program

Branding is a fast-moving world of design, words, and imagery, and the spectrum of applications required by today's brand communications is ever-widening. In the throes of a brand development program, be that a rebrand or merely a brand refresh project, the temptation can be to promise the sun, moon and stars in an attempt to entice and engage a client or to win favor in the white heat of a competitive pitch. On the other hand, beware of causing unnecessary client frustration by under-promising to the point of providing insufficient clarity and definition around the basic essential outputs that the scope of the proposed branding program must deliver. There's a fine line!

To talk in seductive generalities and sound bites when addressing client needs, suggesting creative possibilities and enthusing about ultimate outputs can too often lead to misunderstandings and false expectations of what will be achieved. It is one thing to enthuse and excite a client about the media, marvels and magic of the branding program, but it is quite another for the client to misconstrue talk of ideas and innovations in concept for specific deliverables and outcomes in reality. This is simply storing up problems and disappointment for later in the project when design or creative solutions are being recommended, and the final branding tools, platforms, or applications are being presented for signoff.

To clarify the point, let's imagine some typical examples of the problem:

Proposed activity	Consultant proposes	Client thinks
Video	Create a brand video (meaning an offsite video animation)	Video-filming onsite ("lights, camera, action!")
Visuals	Source visual imagery to support the brand (meaning stock photos)	New original photography, ownable only by the client
Website	Design a new website (meaning a single-page scroll-down brochure type)	A complex, interactive website with multipages and drop-down menus and social media messaging
Copywriting	Create a new brand tagline plus sample brochure copy	A brand tagline plus all brochure copy plus all website copy
Social media	Set up a LinkedIn page plus Twitter presence and an initial blog platform	Set up all social media, including Facebook, Instagram, Pinterest …
Training	A video-based digital user training session for direct platform users	Digital training delivered onsite for the whole marketing team
Planning	A high-level brand and communications plan	A strategic and tactical communications plan with schedules and budgets
Meetings	At key project points plus final senior presentation	On demand, for regular senior team feedback
Reporting	By teleconference and slide presentation	By teleconference plus regular written memo plus final written report
Signoff	By the CX and senior client director and team lead	By the full board plus selected stakeholders

Clearly, it is in the interest of the principal consultant and consulting team presenting to temper enthusiasm and enticement with a clear and sure understanding of what is to be delivered at the end of the project and, equally importantly, what is not. For the sake of clarity and comprehension, a statement of inclusions *and exclusions* should be presented in a written project proposal document and confirmed with the client team or decision maker in advance of commencement to ensure full understanding and agreement.

Initial scoping of the research and strategy phases of a brand project may be as clear as day and very quantified, but the later phases relating to the subsequent generation of eventual creative deliverables (such as those indicated in the preceding table) may remain appealing and aspirational, but as yet merely indicative and still undefined. It is vital to pursue a definition of these final outputs and responsibilities in advance of contractual agreement and project commencement.

At the very least, it is essential to quantify from the very beginning what can and will be tangibly delivered in terms of creative outputs and obligations. Not only is it crucial to be clear on these ultimate commitments, but in doing so, it is sensible and smart to under-promise the outcomes and to over-deliver at project completion and so guarantee high client satisfaction levels and a heightened sense of value of what the consulting and creative team has achieved.

Brand Decision Making Depends Not Only on Operational Stakeholders But Also Political Stakeholders. Engage Both.

Of course, the key decisions about brands (and marketing) are all about the customer, market, and competitive position to take, along with the goals, timing, and investment to make. This is all strictly branding and marketing stuff requiring finger-on-the-pulse customer knowledge, market insights, competitor information, and expertise in market trends and forecasting. On such competences and disciplines are market changes read, alternative plans displayed, and brand decisions made. It's empirical, inspirational, and even emotional stuff and requires having your best branding brains at the table to challenge, cajole, and create the next big idea and values set and visionary way ahead for the brand. These are typically the functional, divisional, and departmental marketing and branding specialists in large companies, the sales manager and managing director in medium-sized companies, or the business owner in small businesses or new start-ups. Such operational stakeholders are, of course, vital to the brand planning and sign-off process, but frequently they are not enough. The fact of the matter is that brand decisions must ultimately come to the boardroom table for presentation, challenge, and approval. This means that executives within the leadership team who are not marketing operational—who are not skilled in branding and marketing—will get their say at least late in the day, and certainly at the end of the process during final decision making about strategy, branding, and funding. These are the political (nonoperational) stakeholders in the brand program who, while not being directly involved in the developmental side of the project, will be required to endorse its outcomes—the recommendations, plans, and designs being proposed for sanction and spend.

They typically include for example the financial controller, production director and IT director, as well as any number of strategic advisors, nonexecutive directors, general stakeholders, and major shareholders who can present themselves in the final reckoning and prove to be either a boon or a barrier to project signoff and creative implementation.

A strategy for endorsement and signoff needs to recognize that these political influencers matter, and it needs to explicitly identify them where possible and as early as possible during the course of the work. The project leadership needs to engage with these important influencers and listen for and to their sincerely and strongly held opinions, aspirations, and expectations. Whether they be actively supporting or merely questioning or even railing against the direction, momentum, or rationale of the creative direction, such influencers must be prehandled sensitively yet emphatically in advance of final decision making and in the interests of keeping the project delivery both on goal and on schedule. Ignore any such political commentators, influencers, or agitators at your peril, or more specifically, at the project's peril—they may possibly even prove to be ultimate decision makers. Engage early and fully to involve them, to prehandle their objections, to inform their perspectives, and to bestow on them a sense of ownership through participation. If they are resistant or cynical, the aim is to convert them from project foe to project friend; if they are receptive or supportive, nurture this and inject enthusiasm and pride to bolster and build their positive disposition and creative perspective. In all cases, be prepared, tread carefully, and assume nothing in advance. At the end of the day, you of course want everyone to be onboard, including both operational and political stakeholders.

Brand Logo Is Not the End Goal. External–Internal Brand Alignment Is.
Your Competitive Market Positioning Depends on It

Let me say this one more time: logo is never the brand goal, and design
is not an end in itself. A brand logo is a tool to express, or to at least say
something about, a brand's uniqueness. It in itself is never the end goal. A
brand is not about a logo; it is about a delivered experience and a developed relationship with the target customer and the broader market—a
relationship based on innovation and value-add. For that brand–customer
relationship to be valid and sustainable, it must be aligned. This means
that the intention and behavior of the brand owner (the company) must
be understood and embraced by the brand buyer (the customer). Where
close alignment is achieved (and assuming customer relevance is high),
this credits the brand with strong customer appeal and market power;
where external–internal alignment is reduced or poor, this weakens the
brand's power and market credibility accordingly. It is key for the brand-
owner to get the brand message out in terms of market innovation, points
of difference, and competitive benefits. Then, the brand's message or
proposition must be received, understood, and (crucially) seen to be relevant by the target audience. This alignment of internal brand intent and
external market understanding will determine the nature and strength of
the brand's competitive advantage in the market, and the degree of this
unity of brand purpose and perception will dictate the ongoing sustainability of that competitive position over time.

Brand Awareness Is Not Enough. Brand Understanding Is Necessary If Brand
Behavior Is to Change. Brand Experience Is Always the Holy Grail

I think it is important to make the point that brand awareness is not the
goal of a brand development program. Brand experience is. The reason I
make the point is that, so often, people in a business will state that what
is important to them is brand awareness—that they want their brand
awareness increased. But awareness of what? Is there a brand strategy in
place? Have the brand values been defined? Is there a governing brand
proposition at hand to convey to the market? And what does company X's
brand stand for anyway? Don't get me wrong, brand awareness is indeed a
vital and treasured asset for any brand, as long as the brand in question …

1. Actually is a brand—and not just a product or service offering
2. Has been defined in terms of values, personality, and proposition
3. Has been audited for current meaning, positioning, and competitive performance
4. Is supported by a developed brand strategy to guide it toward maximizing its future potential

Brand awareness will not deliver business advantage if the understanding associated with the brand is inept or inaccurate. Indeed, brand awareness may be the last thing desired if the brand has developed a negative reputation among users or consumers. Assuming that the latter does not apply, then it is essential that the understanding of the brand and its proposition becomes strong in the market. Achieving this presupposes that the brand has been thoroughly and objectively researched and defined, and that an associated brand strategy is in place, guiding the planning and execution of market communications.

Brand awareness will not on its own guarantee brand understanding, and brand understanding is crucial if market behaviors are to change in favor of brand purchase, trial, and consumption. The more the market really understands the functional and emotional values and advantages that the brand offers, the more powerful the brand will be in winning customer loyalty and share of purse. Understanding, not awareness, drives behavioral change. In this sense, awareness is the lowest goal denomination (that people have heard of the brand), understanding is much higher (what people believe about the brand), and behavior is higher still (how people act or react to the brand offer).

Understanding, not awareness, drives behavioral change.

Ultimately, the ongoing *experience* of the brand in the market is the key determinator of customer behavior and understanding, and in this sense, great brand experience is indeed the Holy Grail of all brand ambition. Managing and increasing brand awareness comes importantly into play to communicate and sustain the positive brand benefits and unique experience that only brand X can deliver. In this way, growing brand awareness is a powerful and vital competitive weapon. Without, however, a defined, understood, and confident brand experience to serve, brand awareness is likely to be an impotent if not risky activity to engage in.

Brand Implementation Does Not Just Happen. Strategy Is About "The Know" and Communication Is About "The Go." But It All Starts Internally.

Brand(ing) is two words not one, as I like to say, meaning that *brand* is the idea and *ing* is communicating it: so branding means communicating an idea. The brand piece is rooted in customer insight, competitive positioning, values definition, and market proposition—so it's all about knowledge, thinking, and strategy; the communicating piece, on the other hand, is all about action: designing, messaging, digital platforms, marketing tools, communicating—brand strategy is about *the know*; communications is about *the go*! In a word: implementation. And it all starts internally. Action stations must take over from deliberations, and the head of steam gathered during the research and strategy stages will not on its own carry the brand through to in-company activation or market trial. That takes an implementation action program, and this does not just happen because there is a sassy and savvy brand strategy in hand.

So, how does a brand get implemented? The secret is to start internally. It must firstly be implemented inside the company. That's key, so the employees and departmental/divisional teams all *get it*, are comfortable with it, and integrate it into their internal communications and behaviors. Company-wide endorsement, engagement, and expression of its unique proposition and values are a must before the brand (new brand or refreshed/evolved brand) can be credibly messaged and communicated in the marketplace. So, the starting place is an internal awareness and engagement objective. This is enabled by setting up the structure and mechanics to support and achieve the introduction of the brand internally across the employee base. (This is discussed in more detail later under Internalizing Branding.)

Brands Should Be Celebrated Before They Are Calculated

Celebration is a key strategy in business. It helps people become motivated by recognizing their talents, efforts, and achievements. This also applies to brands. The managers and staff within the company who lead and are responsible for the brand will become motivated if they are recognized for what they are doing, for what they are striving to achieve, and for the skills and talents that they collectively bring to create brand success. Only in this way, in celebrating what is afoot, what is new, what is creative, will the brand team become motivated and the brand given every possibility of maximum market success. But the temptation for companies can be to act differently, and particularly if there is confusion about the difference between a product and a brand.

You can calculate product sales today—or at least in the immediate to short term—but you cannot calculate brand image, reputation shift, or market positioning in the same way. Product or service sales can be calculated by quantifying the movement of sales units through market channels at a monetary value per unit within a defined sales period. Brand development cannot. A brand is assessed on recognition, relevance, and competitive market position, and it takes time for a new brand to be positioned in a market or for an existing brand to be repositioned. Brand positioning—the process of establishing or strengthening brand relevance in a defined market—is not a short-term tactic; it is by its nature a longer-term strategy.

Brand positioning—the process of establishing or strengthening brand relevance in a defined market—is not a short-term tactic; it is by its nature a longer-term strategy.

Product sales figures do not equate necessarily to brand success or failure; a brand must be judged on other qualitative criteria, including awareness, understanding, relevance, and consumer behavioral response. A brand strategy and development program is not for the short-haul, and as such, it should not be subject to early or hasty quantitative calculations. Early or impatient calculations will not do justice to the potential for competitive positioning and will only act to stifle enthusiasm, confidence, and belief in the project. Better to focus time and effort on celebrating the innovativeness of the brand initiative, its creative endeavor, its visionary journey, its transformation potential, and the opportunities it brings for the company as a whole, for the employee base and for the brand leadership and management team. Celebrate rather than calculate. Or, at least place the focus on celebration in the early stages of brand development while biding the necessary time until qualitative results (brand positioning) can be determined, analyzed, and reported on. In tandem with this, quantitative results (brand-related sales) can then also be assessed and attributed in order to demonstrate brand effectiveness against targets.

So, brand effectiveness should and must be calculated, but in the meantime, and from the get go, brand innovation should and must be celebrated. Celebration will admit and admire all that is visionary and creative and talented about the organization and, in so doing, will set up the right conditions to foster intrinsic motivation across the company and the brand team. In this way, celebration before calculation will promote the likelihood of brand success and will ensure maximum return on the committed brand investment.

Internalizing Branding

Prioritize People and Culture: Balance Brand Design Development With Internal Employer–Brand Investment

I once heard that marketing is about three things: customers, customers, customers! In the same vein, branding could be said to be about three things: reputation, reputation, reputation! But what is reputation without people? Nothing! Reputation cannot exist without people; it is carried in their heads; brand reputation is not out there in the firmament, existing in some separate dimension from human perception; it exists within the perceptual collateral of the human mind. People own brands, clients don't—at least not in a perceptual or consumer loyalty sense. Brands live in people's heads ... in their minds, not in company boardrooms. Related to this, in a recent business meeting, I stated with some conviction that "corporate culture is the commitment, over time, of people to the brand." What I meant was that every organization stands for something—that's its values; its values are its brand, and *living those* is what shapes its culture and its reputation both inside and outside the organization.

> *Corporate culture is the commitment, over time,*
> *of people to the brand.*

Culture is really a prime objective of true brand planning; in my experience, it usually feels outside the reach of most organizations, even those that say they are, and work at being, brand-led. For a compelling, distinctive culture to exist and persist, the values of the brand must be truly embedded in the organization, and deeply so. To achieve this, there can be no *dark corners* or *stones unturned* where the brand values are not communicated, not recognized, not understood, not acted upon. Culture demands consistent and heartfelt, even passionate and certainly emotional, engagement by the people of the organization to the business, its brand values, proposition, and corporate vision. Brand is a no-holds-barred struggle against separatism, contradiction, commoditization, and inconsistency within business and corporate life. It is pro-communication, pro-consistency, pro-creativity, pro-teamwork, and pro-a common purpose. It demands and must have people power: the support of the people within the organization—brand supporters, brand endorsers, brand influencers, brand ambassadors, brand champions, and not just among the titular brand managers, brand executives, or brand directors, but vitally, right across the full panorama of the business, among all and every employee, staff member, colleague, and owner.

In *What Great Brands Do: The Seven Brand-Building Principles That Separate the Best From the Rest* (Yohn 2014), a relentless focus on people engagement and empowerment is presented as the key to activating and sustaining a stand-out brand culture. The author is unequivocal in making the connection between brand, culture, and employee support, stating that: "Operationalizing your brand through company culture requires a focus on design, empowerment, and impact. You want to design the organization and its business model so it delivers on the brand values and attributes. You want to empower your people with the tools and resources to infuse the brand into their day-to-day decisions and behaviors. Finally, you want to make such a positive impact on your employees' lives and their careers that they support your brand's message and mission because they know their own destinies and your brand's destiny are intertwined. One mark of a great brand is that even former employees remain proud to say they helped make the brand great."

Brand performance, effectiveness, and success depend first of all on the people inside the company inculcating the brand at an emotional level—taking it to heart and acting upon it rather than (as is so often assumed) merely relying on design expressing it in the market. In summary, brand experience is an all-encompassing endeavor that balances internal companywide culture with external design-based communications.

A total brand experience depends on an emotional if not passionate embrace of the expressed company brand values and how these are *lived* right across the people base of the organization. People live the brand; design merely communicates it. If people set a high *belief bar* for the brand, then design can rise to that and do it justice through creative expression and communication internally and in the market; if, however, the internal belief bar is set low, then design is constrained and necessarily hidebound in what it can credibly represent, express, and convey (else the brand will quickly disappoint and be found out!). The thesis here is that not only does *culture eat strategy for lunch* but that *culture eats design for dessert!* Culture is king in the world of brand engagement and experience; it is, in fact, the proof of the living of a brand inside an organization. How do you recognize great culture? By seeing and experiencing the passion and positive emotion with which the people base of the organization embraces, understands, regards, talks about and acts upon the brand values and proposition annunciated by the company, throughout the company, for the company.

A *living the brand* approach, standard, and program, therefore, are vital to engendering and sustaining a deep and meaningful and transformative brand culture and holistic corporate experience. A *living the brand* internal employer–brand investment should and must be implemented in balance with investment in design development and creative execution. The promise and expectations that design sets up visually must be matched by the brand experience that follows through to the customer via the people and the culture of the organization, and by its communications, products, services, and value offer. Prioritizing people is essential to building and maintaining a strong brand culture, which, in conjunction with balanced design development and creative expression, will strengthen the organization's brand reputation, business effectiveness, and market growth.

Employees Are Essential: Branding's Just Pretty Without People. But Very Powerful With Them Engaged

When you talk about brands, people typically think *logo*. The first thought that people have is usually related to visual identity. They so often think that brands are about the design of logos and colors and shapes—about the external cosmetics—the pretty side of branding. They think about brands from the outside-in rather than from the inside-out. They rarely consider the central place of people—of employees—in making a brand great. Of course, we want consumers in the marketplace to engage with and experience the brand, but way before this, it is essential to get employees themselves on board and on brand, believing and passionate about the brand, its proposition, and what it seeks to achieve.

Employees are essential to brands, as they are the first line of belief and engagement with the idea and innovation that underpins the brand promise and identity. Indeed, so much of the credibility of a brand rests with the brand owner's employees as their belief and commitment will signal whether, and to what extent, the *brand talk* has real substance and engenders real loyalty inside the company. Internal brand endorsement is the first proof point of a brand's innovativeness and relevance; it is here among employees that the brand owner must work to create awareness and understanding, adoption and enthusiasm, even passion and excitement. If there is a lack of energy for the brand across the employee base, then this augurs poorly for its likely cut-through, perception, and performance in the marketplace. Employees are, in an important sense, a preliminary audience for the brand, but much more significantly, they are potential, and indeed necessary, champions of the brand concept and ambassadors of the brand experience. Brand authenticity and credibility start inside the company and must be felt and accepted in all the far reaches of the organization if it is to be received with confidence in the market.

> *Internal brand endorsement is the first proof point of a*
> *brand's innovativeness and relevance.*

It is of paramount importance, therefore, that the brand owner or senior management team achieves effective internalization of the brand right across the company. When employees are *living the brand* in this way and enthusiastically adopting its values and attributes into their ways of working and behavior, then the real power of the brand can be truly seen and felt. Brands are essentially and primarily catalysts for behavioral change in the face of positive, value-adding innovation. With employees endorsing and integrating new brand-based behaviors, then the full power and potential of a brand can be experienced; with brand champions extolling the merits of the brand internally and brand ambassadors communicating its customer virtues externally, then and only then can the full power of branding be observed, understood, and appreciated. People, not logo design, make brands powerful.

Activate a "Living The Brand" Program. Prioritize Your Mechanics of Change

The mechanics for brand introduction or evolution will, of course, vary from company to company, but some classic approaches are highlighted in Figure 2.3, which include the establishment of a brand council, the furnishing of a *brand room,* nomination of brand ambassadors/team leaders (natural brand champions are preferred here), the setup of an online brand information hub, a brand roadshow, and the systemization of brand touchpoint monitoring.

A word on each of these…..

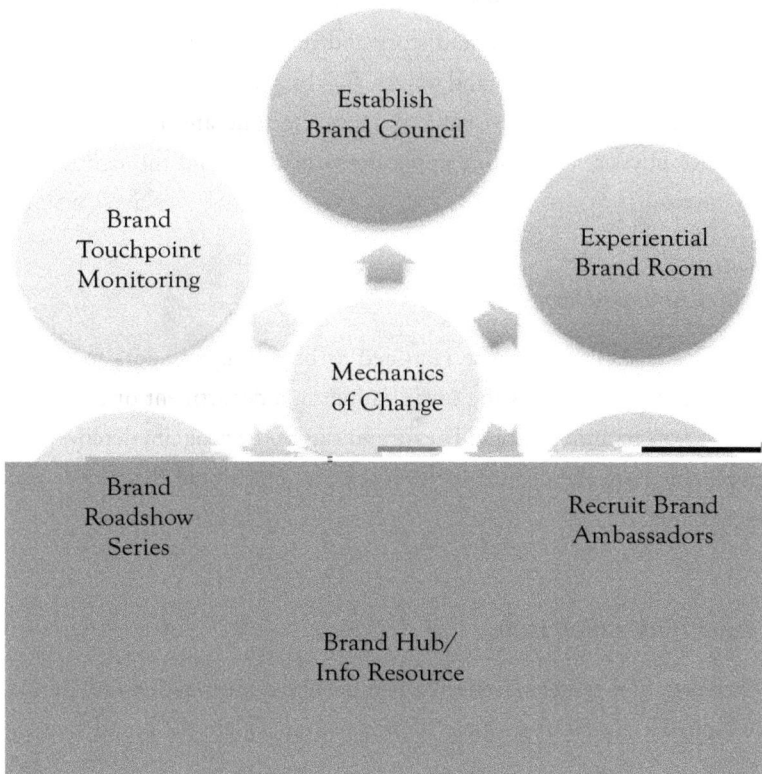

Figure 2.3 Living the brand—mechanics of change

Brand Council

A brand council is a handpicked group of company leaders who take the responsibility for the rollout of the new brand and its communications both inside and outside the company. The brand council comprises all key executive brand stakeholders and will include the brand strategy consultant with periodic inputs from senior creatives on a need-be basis. The brand council sets implementation objectives and monitors progress en route whilst all the time reviewing goals, actions, and tactics and making or approving decisions on priorities, messaging, resourcing, and outcomes.

Brand Room

A *brand room* is a walk-in branded sensory environment. It is where the brand proposition and personality are proudly introduced, displayed, interpreted, and experienced in a dedicated three-dimensional space. This brings reality to the brand story and promise, and confidently and creatively manifests the brand values and brand personality. This facility shows off the brand visually and sets the tone and benchmark for all other physical and online applications of the brand throughout the organization.

Brand Ambassadors

Team leaders should also be recruited as brand ambassadors to champion the initiative across the organization on a department or divisional basis. These become the brand's eyes and ears as the program deploys, and employees have the chance to feedback and contribute their ideas and suggestions.

Brand Information Hub

In support of these team leaders, an online brand information hub should be created as a central resource to present and explain the brand strategy and its implementation goals. This would also encourage personal commentary and be fully accessible on the company website (such as via a micro-site with passport access to protect privacy). This online resource would act as a continuous brand forum of ongoing progress reports, performance metrics, visual manifestations of brand messaging, promotion of brand events, postings of employee Q&As, and so on … . It would promote the brand program, its goals, deployment, resourcing, and effectiveness.

Brand Roadshows

To deepen understanding and demonstrate personal company leadership and CEO commitment, a series of brand roadshows is a powerful action to take. These allow senior management and business owners to get face-to-face with their employees who would be *living the brand*. The senior leadership team would endorse the strategic importance of the brand project for the company (and for its future profitability and employment security), as well as demonstrating the purpose, passion, and priorities that successful brand positioning in the market will demand. The roadshow program would seek to engage with the entire organization over time and set out examples and expectations of new competitive brand behaviors and performance standards, with belief, passion, and commitment clearly demonstrated by the company leadership team.

Touchpoint Mapping and Monitoring

As aptly and simply defined in *Beyond Advertising: Creating Value Through All Customer Touchpoints* (Wind et al. 2016), "A touchpoint is an opportunity. An encounter. What happens at that moment either paves the way for the next moment of truth or chips away at the value built to date." A mapping out of key customer touchpoints across the organization and its brands would be a priority as and when management seek to identify and understand the hotspots of brand experience. But exactly what and where are these touchpoints and hotspots? They are wherever customers (and prospects) intersect with, or intensely engage with, the company and its brands—at which point the customer experience must match up to the company's promise about its brand values, personality, proposition, and value-add. And as reminded by Kevin McTigue (*Leveraging Touchpoints in Today's Branding Environment*) in *Kellogg on Branding in A Hyper-connected World* (Tybout et al. 2019), leveraging brand touchpoints is ultimately key to driving return on investment. McTigue puts it this way " ... by systematically mapping touchpoints and creating a customer journey based on your target customers' behavior, marketers will be able to understand where to prioritize and focus, which is the key to ROI."

Consequential to this, the monitoring of customer touchpoints and brand hotspots, and the actions taken in response, would become a regular component of a strategy for sustained brand performance, ensuring that the customer experience delivered becomes increasingly consistently on-brand.

At this stage of implementation, the company would now be well in transition to becoming a brand-centric organization where up-to-the-moment performance feedback can be quickly communicated through an online information hub and via a structured brand leadership and brand council management and information system.

With the brand values and performance commitments internalized, visualized, and messaged companywide throughout office, depot, and branch premises, the brand will have been brought to life right across the organization. This would be manifested in both printed and digital format, and the company, departmental teams, and individual employees, be they office or market-based, would be equipped and ready to articulate the brand's promise and uniqueness both inside and outside the organization.

It is such joined-up internal activity along with concerted, consistent action and communications that creates and sustains in-company brand awareness, understanding, and belief. Ultimately, concerted internal communication of the brand combined with effective positioning, messaging, and brand experience in the market will deliver a strong brand reputation and equity for the company, reward and security for the employees, and distinctive value for the customer.

Identify Your Instinctive Internal Brand Champions. Use Their Natural Passion to Evangelize Across the Organization

Brand performance is about people and product rather than graphic design—even though the latter is usually the first thought when brand development is being discussed. Of course, graphic design is important and plays the key role in visually expressing what a brand is about, but it is people who live the brand and love the brand, and nowhere is this truer than inside the company across the employee base. Of course, some employees are immediately attracted to the brand more than others, and in almost an instinctive fashion as they really *get* the brand—its innovation, proposition, values, and excitement. Where brand innovation is really delivering strong brand stand-out and differentiation, then some employees will tune into this very quickly and in an emotional way; they will instinctively be brand champions—or at least be poised to become brand champions with a little help from senior management. I have witnessed this in many industries, and in organizations of all sizes. It reflects an innate loyalty among staff for the company and the nature of its business and corporate values. This then acts as a sure stepping stone to employees companywide to also recognize, accept, and ultimately champion the innovation or quantum step that the new or evolved brand is now making.

So, these internal brand champions get it, are passionate about it, and are ready and willing to be directly involved in promoting the brand throughout the organization, among fellow colleagues and departmental teams. They are a real and treasured asset to any brand and to any business. The asset shows itself in the form of immediate understanding of the brand's innovation, persuasive optimism about the difference the brand will make, pervasive passion in the ingenuity of the company, and personal pride in the resourcefulness of its people. And being naturally passionate about the brand, such champions are immediately willing (or easily encouraged) to evangelize across the organization on behalf of the brand innovation and its potential transformative effect for the company.

In smaller organizations, natural brand champions can be easily and quickly identified by the business leadership team; in larger organizations, they will be nominated by senior management but also by being identified as brand enthusiasts during the course of, for example, cross-company brand roadshows, leadership presentations, information events, or brand implementation workshops (the latter would be run, for example, at and post a brand launch day). However they are identified, such natural brand champions should become fully engaged in an internal brand dissemination and learning program for all employees. In this role, they act as powerful and highly credible voices among their colleagues and peers, being active either within their local corporate environment or by participating in brand engagement events and experiences companywide. Natural brand champions will be thrilled to participate in an internal brand engagement program and are a vital and dynamic way to spread brand awareness, understanding, and fervor.

Recognize. Reward. Celebrate. Brand Success Is a Communal Experience Without Walls. Structure This Into the Annual Calendar

Internalizing the brand experience and inculcating the brand's values throughout the organization is fundamental to sustained brand belief internally and proclaimed brand belief externally. Brand belief must start *at home* and exude from within the company so that all customer touchpoints (every place the customer comes in contact with the company) consistently and faithfully deliver an authentic on-brand experience that builds credibility, belief, and brand loyalty in the market. This makes brand development and brand success very much a communal experience and a communal responsibility, and as I've said elsewhere, some employees will be more naturally instinctive and adept than others at championing the brand.

So, effectiveness in understanding, communicating, and *living* the brand in thought, word and deed is a vital asset, and achieving this across the entire employee base is an obvious prerequisite of brand and company leadership. And as brand guru Nicholas Ind rightly cautions in *Living the Brand*, as documented in *The Definitive Book of Branding* (Kompella 2014): "While the active involvement of leaders is vital to bringing the brand to life especially at a more strategic level, by itself it is insufficient. The brand will lack a deeper relevance if it remains the preserve of a few senior people or only head office employees. People at all levels, business units, functional areas, and geographies, need to have the opportunity to build the brand. Thus, employees need to participate in creating brand meaning and humanizing the abstraction of the brand idea through what they say and do." This means that the brand idea and its precious values must not be regarded as the prized possession of the company leadership team or of a subset of employees; it means that the brand must become democratized throughout the organization to such an extent that everyone feels real ownership and proactive commitment to its delivery at every customer touchpoint. As the prime purpose and unifying idea around which the entire organization is to rally, employee brand belief, loyalty, active support, indeed innovation, must deservedly and fulsomely be recognized, rewarded, and regularly celebrated.

And it's worth making this point emphatically again: there are no walls or boundaries to brand responsibility as it is in everyone's interest that all employees of the company support and faithfully execute brand-led change that strengthens relevance, appeal, and competitive position, and thereby the company's success, profitability, and business security in its served market. The unified support and ambition of the employee base to meet the challenges of brand change and to achieve and maintain market differentiation is always a direct implication of refreshing, evolving, or rebranding a company, its brand, or its brand portfolio. This takes energy, enthusiasm, and efficiency without which a brand campaign must be destined to flounder or even to fail. Fruitful outcomes depend on passion and persistence (and of course a great product), and such internal cross-company commitment must be recognized and rewarded. Celebrating brand effort and success is not only a must-do but also an opportunity to praise the people across the employee base who are not just brand believers but who are enterprising, enthusiastic, even evangelical for brand awareness, performance, and success. Dedication to brand experience delivery is always an internal communal characteristic where brand cut-through and innovation are achieved in the market. Likewise, its celebration must be prioritized and structured into the annual company calendar.

While the brand will ultimately reside in the mind of the customer, in the meantime, it is the company's employees and brand teams who guide, nurture, and creatively cajole the brand to its market positioning, recognition, and enduring effectiveness. Every opportunity should be taken to celebrate brand endeavor and success in reinforcing the brand values at every possible moment and place across the employee base and at all customer touchpoints. This is a leadership imperative that will shape company culture and employee perspectives, making for a truly brand-led organization, a values-based working environment, and a more unified, satisfied, fulfilled, motivated, and happier workforce.

Key Takeaways

Branding is about two things: words and images.

75 percent of what makes a brand great has nothing to do with the product or service delivered.

The brand does not live in the boardroom or the MD's office. It lives in the marketplace.

Don't think branding first. Think brand proposition.

Make sure the creative gets the big idea, not just the written brief.

Qualitative research is essential to brand understanding.

Aim for a strong identity. Be brave with colors and imagery.

Clients do not buy what they do not like. Clients do not buy what they do not understand.

Brand logo is not the end goal. External–internal values alignment is.

Brand awareness is not enough. Brand understanding is necessary if brand behavior is to change.

Prioritize people and culture: balance brand design development with internal employer–brand investment.

Recognize. Reward. Celebrate. Brand success is a communal experience without walls.

The Word Wizard	
Expression	**Explanation**
Brand	Uniqueness you know, want, and trust
Brand behaviors	The behavior, activities, and interaction of those responsible for planning, producing, and promoting the brand
Brand believers	Those who believe that a brand is an effective business and profit driver

The Word Wizard	
Expression	**Explanation**
Brand-centric	The organization of a business around promising and delivering a brand values and culture-based experience to its customer base
Brand champions	Those within the employee base who are instinctively and outstandingly disposed toward, and passionate about, the brand
Brand council	A handpicked leadership team that takes the responsibility for guiding and managing the development, approval, and deployment of a new brand
Brand essence	The ultimate thumbprint of the brand's meaning; the distilled (typically three-word) shorthand for what a brand stands for
Brand forum	A discussion-based in-company workshop session that deeply explores, investigates, and defines pan-organizational beliefs and perceptions
Brand hotspots	Priority points of intense customer connection and engagement with the brand
Brand intent	The vision and endeavor of the brand owner and management team to deliver a values-based brand experience to the customer
Brand loyalty	The ongoing customer trust that a brand enjoys
Brand owner	The ultimate legal owner of the brand (in the company)
Brand performance	The effectiveness and competitive power of the experience that the brand delivers
Brand personality	The style, attitude, and nature of how a brand behaves
Brand portfolio	The range of brands that an organization possesses and markets
Brand position	The understanding that a brand commands about its particular customer relevance and competitive uniqueness
Brand principles	The underlying truths and rules relating to the effective planning and achievement of brand growth and success
Brand resonance	The extent of the reach and impact of a brand in the market
Brand strategy	The plan that guides what the brand is to stand for in order to achieve relevance and competitive differentiation in the market
Brand vision	The strategic intent of how the brand is expected to engage people and the market and impact on consumers' lives

(continued)

The Word Wizard	
Expression	**Explanation**
Communication platforms	The range and variety of channels by which a brand message can be communicated
Competitive positioning	The different proposition that a company makes in the marketplace to achieve competitive advantage; the difference of a company's market offer relative to competitors
Customer touchpoints	The places and points in the buying process where the customer directly interacts with the company
Design execution	The creation of designs for identity development or brand and marketing communication
Emotional	The intangible experience that a brand provides that connects with customers at the nonphysical level
Engagement	The extent to which a customer or an employee believes in and gets involved with the brand both physically and emotionally
Equity	The difference between what something is worth (an asset) and what is owed on it (debt and liabilities)
Iconography	The use of visual imagery and symbols
Inherent values	The underlying, core values on which a brand is based
Internalization	The promotion and embedding of a brand's proposition and values internally across a company's employee base and systems
Management imperative	An absolute priority that management must address
Market positioning	The market sector or customer grouping for whom the brand is recognized to be highly relevant
Marketing collateral	The suite of design applications of the brand's identity for the purpose of presenting the brand and its product and service offer to the market
On-brand	To be in alignment with the brand values and proposition
Points of difference	All and any ways in which the brand, its delivery, and consumption experience, is unique or different from competing brands
Portfolio	A catalog or suite of brands, products, or services
Principles of branding	Underlying truths and rules relating to the effective application of branding as a system of communication and business growth
Proposition	What the brand stands for, believes about itself, and promises to the customer

The Word Wizard	
Expression	Explanation
Qualitative beliefs	The intangible, emotionally based understandings of the differential benefits and experience that a brand offers the market
Qualitative research	Research that is directed (moderated) but unstructured in order to determine perceptions, beliefs, feelings, emotional values, and deep-seated needs
Quantitative characteristics	The components of a brand that are product-focused in nature relating to what it is or what it functionally does
Rational values	Also known as functional values, these relate to physical, practical, nonemotional elements of a brand's offer
Rebranding	The act of replacing an existing corporate or product brand by planning, creating, and implementing an entirely new brand identity
Resonance	The extent of the market reach and impact of a business activity or brand innovation
Served market	A specific part of the total market that a company uniquely serves and in which it has a recognized brand presence
Strategic intent	The vision and endeavor of the senior management team to achieve a particular business goal
Tagline	A copywritten line that is incorporated into a brand identity to support and qualify a logo or a written brand communication
Tone of voice	The character and personality of a brand or a business that is conveyed through the use of words both spoken and written
Value-add	The total additional benefit that a brand provides to the customer
Value offer	The unique and total product value and customer experience that is promised or offered
Value proposition	The promise that a brand makes to its customer in terms of differential benefits, usage experience, and value for money

Experience

Identity and culture run deep: As a company employee, my first branding experience was in the early 1980s when, just graduated and eager to make my mark, I was the marketing manager at linen manufacturer Ulster Weaving Company in Belfast. The *troubles* in Northern Ireland were at their height and UWC was located right in the middle of a renowned loyalist area. The company's logo depicted the Red Hand of Ulster—a politically rooted emblem to say the least—and senior management wisdom at the time was to rebrand the company to something less emotive and more appealing internationally. A thorough, professional brand consulting process was instigated, and external branding experts were engaged to lead and guide a redesign. As a marketing manager, my role was simply to liaise with and facilitate the external consulting team. I had a support role only, and this was my first deep dive into a full rebranding project. The experts made their final recommendations, and the Red Hand logo device was shortly replaced by a logo design based on a field of flax (the plant from whose stalk linen is made). But that was not the final presentation to me. Not at all. Once word got out that the *Red Hand* had been demoted, I got a special visitor. My office door burst open early one morning, and without a word, an anonymous paramilitary gentleman pulled a chair up and stared at me accusingly across my desk: "Are you responsible for getting rid of our Red Hand?" he asked abruptly. "No!" said I decisively and emphatically. A period of mutual silence ensued, and a few threatening mutterings later, I found myself peaceably alone again. I was left in no doubt, however, about the impact of brand identity, the importance of imagery, and the power of the culture of organizations.

Experience
Curate as well as create: So often, I come across companies whose social media just doesn't live up to expectations or to their brand promise. The company website may look fresh, attractive, even compelling, but their social channels—their blog, LinkedIn, Facebook, Twitter, Instagram, ... can be embarrassingly out of date and amazingly out of touch with current issues and trends. It's just not good enough to set up social channels and then fail to regularly curate them. Blogs should not be left untouched for months on end without fresh content and insightful opinion and perspectives shared.

Expertise

No off-the-shelf solutions: Buy as many branding books as you like—including this one!—but the brand development journey will inevitably throw up many unexpected learnings and lessons en route. Prepare and plan as you must, at the end of the day brand-building is a personal experience for everyone involved, and local culture, politics, and preferences will always have an impact. There are no off-the-shelf ready solutions. Go create!

Expertise

Gain the hearts and minds of the key players: Selling the brand project internally from the project get-go is crucial: this means positioning it emphatically with the whole management team—they are the folks who will need to steer, support, and facilitate it through the research and development phases and then be enthusiastic and decisive about it when final creative solutions are being presented. Make friends early and everywhere!

Example

Be and be seen to be the right fit: Getting everyone on board the brand project means also gaining acceptance that the brand team is the right one for the job. I remember consulting with the national division of a global cutting tool saw-grit manufacturer. The chief marketing officer (CMO) engaged us to internalize the brand across its Northern Hemisphere companies by inducting all subsidiary company MDs. We impressed and delivered, and eventually, the global group CEO began to notice us. It was only when we were lined up by the CMO for a rebrand of the global company that the CEO asked "and how many do you have on your team?" Of course he ran with a big, global brand agency, with us retained as the regional player in a supporting role. What is it they used to say ... no one ever got fired for buying IBM! And, by the way, size matters!

CHAPTER 3

What's It Worth?
Valuing Your Brand

Chapter Overview

Valuing a brand is a natural follow-on consideration from establishing and owning a brand. But how is it done, and what are the options? This chapter explores the rationale for financial brand valuation and the conditions for brand value growth, and introduces a range of popular international methods and proprietary measurement approaches. The challenges and complications of valuing a brand are acknowledged, including the ongoing fluctuation in a brand's business and market circumstances, as well as the sheer multitude of possible measurement methodologies. Four published approaches by global brand agencies are examined to provide high-level insight and understanding, namely those of Interbrand, Landor, Kantar Millward Brown, and Brand Finance. To broaden perspective, an overview of additional alternative approaches is also presented.

Why and How to Value a Brand

There is much talk in business circles not only about the effect of a brand on market relevance and market share growth but also on how to value a brand as a discrete sales driver and profit center of the business. The belief here is that a brand is something that can be identified and isolated as a distinct performance-driving asset, providing monetary, market image, and goodwill benefits for which a financial value can be specifically calculated. *The International Brand Valuation Manual* (Salinas 2009) identifies the Rank Hovis McDougall (RHM) brand valuation in 1988 as being the very first brand valuation, stating that "the majority of academics in the field locate the birth of the brand valuation industry in this event." Beyond this, Salinas attributes the roots and origins of brand valuation methods more generally to a wider series of major corporate acquisitions, advising that: "The series of brand acquisitions in the late 1980s revealed the hidden value of companies with strong brands, and generated growing interest in brand valuation." To support this, a case example is provided: "When the British company GrandMet acquired Pillsbury in 1988, it paid an estimated 88% of the price as goodwill (*Understanding the Financial Value of Brands*, Haigh 1999). Since then, other acquisitions have shown that brands can create value and justify high market-to-book multiples ...(and) the overall trend was that acquisition prices for companies with strong brands were consistently higher than the value of their net tangible assets."

Now fast-forward to 2011, when ex-P&G CEO Jim Stengel published the findings of his 10-year growth study (2001–2011) of more than 50,000 brands around the world. Based on the outcome of his analysis (in partnership with brand firm Millward Brown Optimor), Stengel makes the case emphatically for the irrefutable role of brand-based growth in great businesses. In his book *Grow: How Ideals Power Growth and Profit at the World's 50 Greatest Companies* (2011), he states that: "In 1980 virtually the entire market capitalisation of the S&P 500 [Standard & Poor 500] companies consisted of tangible assets (cash, offices, plants, equipment, inventories, etc.). In 2010 tangible assets accounted for only 40 to 45 percent of the S&P 500 companies' market capitalisation. The rest of their capitalisation consisted of intangible assets, and about half of that—more than 30 percent of total market capitalisation—came from brand. The growth in the importance of brand value over the last thirty years is unmistakable." And then Stengel continues by adamantly insisting that "brand value is now most companies' single biggest asset, and the consequence is that business leadership and brand leadership are converging in every industry and every sector of the economy. The world's best companies have responded to this by ensuring that they bring together business leadership and brand leadership in the c-suite and throughout their organisations." As if further elaboration were needed, Stengel also summarizes that "Businesses are now only as strong as their brands, and nothing else offers business leaders so much potential leverage. This is why I believe every business leader—whether you are selling cars, chemicals, or cosmetics—needs to think and act like a brand leader."

Today, it is now widely accepted that strong brands play a significant role in driving business performance. This is because they are proven to have a direct influence on current customers, prospective customers, employees, and investors. They are powerful in attracting prospects, increasing customer loyalty, retaining employed talent, and contributing to a more secure and sustainable business into the future. Ultimately, the economic value of a brand—what it is worth to the business—is a measure of its power to maintain and grow competitive advantage by generating new customer demand, by sustaining business activity over time, and by reducing investment risk.

Strong brands play a significant role in driving business performance.

But what is a brand worth? This is the inevitable question that must eventually dawn on all brand owners, stakeholders, managers, practitioners: what is my brand worth? What value can I place on it? Valuing a brand is, of course, just like valuing a business: the market value will be a direct function of market demand: no demand, no value; high demand, high value ... no matter what the value of the production assets in hand or the marketing investment to date. In other words, the stronger a brand is perceived to be by the market, the more competitively powerful it is, and therefore, the more commercially valuable it is.

Ultimately, the calculation of brand worth (also called brand equity or brand asset value) derives from the extent to which a brand can be proven to deliver economic value to the business. That's how important brands are, and that's why they accrue value—but how precisely can you measure that? Business people talk about brand value, brand power, and brand equity all the time—the value of the business that is directly attributable to their proprietary brand or brand portfolio. And of course, it's volatile—it's constantly changing with the seasons, the trends, the innovations, the level of competition. Figure 3.1 defines what creates brand power and brand equity, and Figure 3.2 illustrates how brand equity comprises the accumulation of brand value across a company at corporate brand, sub-brand, and product brand levels.

The Equation of Brand Power

Distinctive Values	+	Relevant Propositions	×	Market Adoption	=	Brand Power

The Equation of Brand Equity

Market Adoption	×	Market Size	×	Brand Loyalty	=	Brand Equity

Figure 3.1 Equations of brand power and brand equity

The preceding equations show that brand power is created by market adoption of relevant propositions and distinctive values, but that brand equity is achieved through market size and brand loyalty, and thereby sustained consumer advocacy and profit-generating repeat purchase.

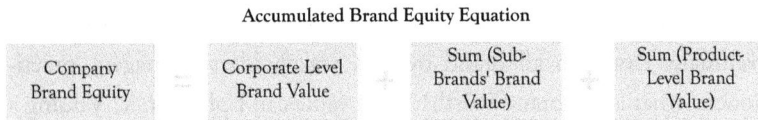

Accumulated Brand Equity Equation

Company Brand Equity	=	Corporate Level Brand Value	+	Sum (Sub-Brands' Brand Value)	+	Sum (Product-Level Brand Value)

Figure 3.2 Accumulated brand equity equation

The preceding equation underlines that companywide brand equity is the accumulation of brand asset value at corporate, sub-brand, and product levels. Corporate level accounts for the asset value of the overall company (parent) brand itself; sub-brand level accounts for the asset value of the specified and planned brands within the sub-brand structure of the organization; product-level brands account for the asset value of any product or service brands that may have developed at the product level as individual market offerings outside of the sub-brand structure.

The challenge of valuing a brand is not merely concerned with knowing the extent of demand for a brand in the market—sales forecasting and market share growth can indicate that. Rather, it's about the intricacies of calculating brand value in hard financial terms. Ultimately, it's an accounting exercise. Most people might well know that a particular brand is very valuable—because it has fantastic awareness and is in great demand—but accounting procedures and financial models are then necessary to place a defined, explicit monetary value on the economic asset that the brand represents.

The starting article of faith must be that a brand adds value and does so to exponentially greater effect than a mere product or service, but the question is how to go about valuing that, how to value in real money the emotional bond and the experiential distinctiveness that a brand possesses and provides. Valuing a product, therefore, is one thing (the tangible/functional), valuing a brand is quite another (the intangible/emotional).

Valuing a product analyzes the physical makeup, features, and components on offer; it is a calculation of its component parts and their performance in solving a functional need. But as John Stuart once famously stated when he was Chairman of Quaker Oats Ltd: "If this business were to be split up, I would be glad to take the brands, trademarks, and goodwill, and you could have all the bricks and mortar—and I would fare better than you" (*Understanding, Measuring, and Using Brand Equity*, Dyson et al. 1996).

Valuing a brand is about valuing the intangible, the emotional, the physically unquantifiable, and this is where the rub comes: how do you value what is not physical but yet is so clearly real, relevant, and resonant in the consumer's mind and is recognized as a distinctive experience in and by the market? How to account for that? Figure 3.3 shows the key influencing factors to be taken into account.

The challenge of accounting for the intangible asset that is a trust-based business-to-customer relationship is then further complicated by many other dynamics, variables, and uncontrollables such as a changing competitive landscape, market seasonality, media sensitivity, volatile economic conditions, fickle consumer demand, disruptive social change, international politics!

But a stand has to be taken at a point in time of strategic necessity or importance that, subject to the prevailing market conditions and demand realities, a brand should be allocated a specific monetary value. Different analytical methodologies are, of course, going to produce different monetary results. In addition, valuation calculations will be directly influenced by changing market and economic realities at different points in time. Furthermore, the final agreed valuation will depend also on the level of personal interest, intent, or implacable resolve of a prospective buyer to acquire the brand or, indeed, of the seller to achieve an exit strategy.

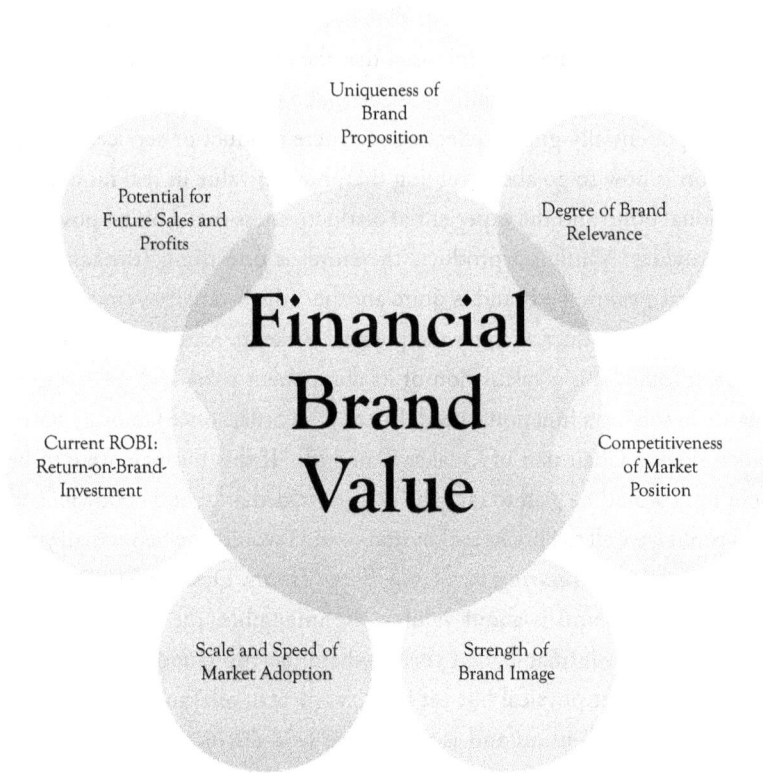

Figure 3.3 Key influencing factors in brand valuation

The preceding model identifies seven key influencing factors that have a direct effect on the financial value of a brand. The model is based on brand relevance, market adoption, and the expectation of future sales and profits. The greater the uniqueness and relevance of a brand proposition and its competitiveness in the market, combined with strength of brand image among target customers, and their scale and speed of brand adoption, will determine current sales and return-on-brand-investment to date. Similarly, brand performance to date will inform expectations of future sales and profit potential and related return-on-brand-investment into the future.

And, never mind the variables and uncontrollables of the market or the personal disposition of the buyer, the most obvious challenge confronting brand valuation is the sheer multitude and diversity of possible measurement methodologies—some consumer-based, some financial-based, some composite-based, some hard measurement-based (quantitative), some soft measurement-based (qualitative).

The most obvious challenge confronting brand valuation is the sheer multitude and diversity of possible measurement methodologies.

In *The International Brand Valuation Manual* (2009), Salinas describes the three general ways in which a brand asset—indeed any kind of asset—can be valued, namely the cost, market or income approach, with the Author summarizing the nature of each approach as follows:

The Cost Approach

With the cost approach, the brand is valued by considering the cost of developing it (brand acquisition, creation, or maintenance) during any and all phases of its development (testing, product concept R&D, product improvements, promotions).

The Market Approach

The market approach considers recent transactions (sales, acquisitions, licenses, etc.) that have involved similar brands and for which data regarding the transaction price is available.

The Income Approach

The income approach requires the identification of future income, profits, or cash flow attributable to the brand over its expected remaining useful life, and discounting or capitalizing them to present value. In order to arrive at a capital value, the estimated future cash flows or earnings attributable to the brand are discounted back to present value (*Discounted Cash Flows*) or multiplied by a capitalization factor (*Direct Capitalization*).

Having described the characteristics and various options of applying each general approach, Salinas also proceeds to adjudicate on their applicability. She cautions that: "the cost method, in any of its variants, is not appropriate for brand valuation. It is more commonly applied in cases of easily replaceable assets, such as software or customer databases." She concludes that "the market approach is ideal for valuing assets that are not unique. In the case of brands, this approach may be applied—*though not as a primary method*—to calculate fair value or value in use when the transaction involves a similar brand in the same industry." In which case, Salinas is identifying *the income approach* as the prime arbiter of brand valuation, although not necessarily in the form of an exclusive, standalone methodology, but rather with the market approach ideally providing supporting perspective as much as possible.

In addition, in a further wide-ranging review of existing international valuation thinking, *Methods of Brand Evaluation* (Bulgarelli 2015) defines and identifies four overall alternative brand valuation approaches: consumer, financial, formulary, and composite. These can be summarized as follows:

Consumer-Based Approaches

A consumer-based approach proposes that brand value exists whenever customers' preferences for a brand are greater than what the simple assessment of the utility of the product attributes would have suggested. One approach here (the conversion method) is to estimate and value the level of brand awareness that was needed in order to achieve the current sales turnover. Another approach (the customer preference method) is to calculate the value of the brand by matching an increase in awareness to the corresponding increase in market share.

Financial-Based Approaches

A financial-based approach is where the brand is regarded as a conditional asset, meaning that for a brand to produce a profit or economic value added (EVA), a tangible base and product or service is needed. The brand is seen as an added value after having allowed for the capital required for its production and for the cost of other intangible assets that have contributed to the business. Once all the directly valuable assets have been factored in, the residual derived will create the economic value for the brand (and for other intangibles that cannot easily be evaluated directly). As per the options presented above by Salinas for brand asset valuation, the same three main approaches are again identified here:

- A cost-based approach—where the brand is valued according to the cost of developing it.
- A market-based approach—where the brand value is estimated by reference to open market values.
- An income-based approach—where the value of the brand is dictated by the future expected cash flows that will be attributable directly to the brand itself.

Formulary Approaches

A formulary approach is where specialized proprietary formulae are applied to determine brand valuation. Examples are the Financial World Magazine method—this estimates the premium profit attributable to the brand by subtracting the earnings of a comparable unbranded product from the branded operating profit;, and the Brand Equity Ten method—which evaluates customer loyalty, perceived quality or leadership, customer associations about perceived value and brand personality and organization characteristics, and awareness and market behavior relating to market share, market price and distribution coverage.

Composite Approaches

A composite approach is where various economic and behavior-oriented valuation methods are utilized such as the Integrated Model of Brand Valuation method, which combines the economic, psychographic, behavioral, and composite brand valuation methods. This approach categorizes the key analytical factors into three separate groups: brand strength factors, brand image factors, and brand defense and conflict factors. These factors are ranked, and a weighted index is applied to reflect the relative importance of each group.

It is not surprising that such different and wide-ranging approaches deliver different brand valuations—what is surprising is the huge variation that can occur in the monetary values resulting. For example, three widely accepted methodologies—those of Kantar Millward Brown, Brand Finance, and Interbrand—have valued the Apple brand at $301 billion (2018), $146 billion (2018) and $184 billion (2017) respectively. Similarly, Google could be worth $302 billion, $121 billion or $142 billion depending on which methodology is used! (Sources: *BrandZ Top 100 Most Valuable Global Brands 2018*, Kantar Millward Brown; *Global 500 2018*, Brand Finance; *Best Global Brands 2017*, Interbrand.)

Ultimately, like any business, a brand is worth what someone wants to pay for it at any given moment in time, and a diverse range of *proprietary* accounting methods have been developed to determine what that monetary value should be. To enhance understanding, the following outlines provide insights into bespoke applied approaches, as expounded by four leading global brand agencies: Interbrand, Landor, Kantar Millward Brown, and Brand Finance:

Interbrand talks about a brand strength-based valuation comprising:
(Source: *Brand Valuation, A Versatile Strategic Tool for Business*)

Three key components to brand valuation:	A. Financial brand performance B. Role of brand (in the purchase decision) C. Brand strength (*)

(*) with brand strength being assessed via an evaluation of 10 key factors (internal and external) as follows:

Internal factors:	Clarity, commitment, protection, responsiveness
External factors:	Authenticity, relevance, differentiation, consistency, presence, understanding

Landor talks about softer measurements of brand valuation comprising:
(Source: *Stop the Chest Beating: The End of Monetary Brand Valuation*)

• Measuring the ability of a brand to deliver the future business (future-proofing)
• Measuring the impact of a brand on experiences, (digital) interactions, (social) conversations
• Measuring how much these experiences align with both current and future customer expectations
• Measuring branded interactions to anticipate future customer needs and purchase drivers

Kantar Millward Brown talks about a brand contribution-based valuation comprising:

(Source: *BrandZ Valuation Methodology*)

Three key phases in the valuation process:	A. Calculating the financial value B. Calculating the brand contribution C. Calculating the brand value

These comprise eight distinct process steps as follows:

1. Apportion earnings of the corporation across a portfolio of brands (where of course the company owns more than one brand)
2. Attribute the correct portion of earnings to each brand by analyzing financial information to define the attribution rate
3. Multiply corporate earnings by the attribution rate to show branded earnings (the amount of corporate earnings attributed to a particular brand)
4. Determine the brand multiple—the brand's future earnings prospects as a multiple of current earnings
5. Determine the financial value—assess the branded value of the business by multiplying the brand earnings by the brand multiple (this defines the amount of the total value of the corporation that is attributable specifically to its brand/s)
6. Measure 3 key brand associations: *Meaningful, Different,* and *Salient*: meaningful (a combination of emotional and rational affinity); different (the extent to which it is, or feels, different to consumers); salient (the extent to which it comes to mind quickly and easily as the right purchase choice)
7. Define the brand contribution—the unique role played by the brand in delivering purchase volume along with any extra price premium delivered by these brand associations
8. Calculate brand value—multiply financial value by brand contribution (expressed as a percentage of the financial value). Brand value is defined here as the monetary amount that a brand contributes to the overall value of a corporation or business

Brand Finance talks about a royalty relief-based valuation approach:

(Source: *Global 500 2018, The Annual Report on the World's Most Valuable Brands*)

The royalty relief approach estimates the likely future revenues attributable to a brand	It calculates a royalty rate that would be charged for its use. This determines a brand valuation that is understood as the net economic benefit that a licensor would achieve by licensing the brand in the open market

This approach comprises seven distinct steps as follows:

1.	Calculate the brand strength by using a balanced scorecard of metrics, which specifically assess market investment, stakeholder equity, and business performance
2.	Determine the royalty range for each industry, reflecting the importance of brand to purchasing decisions (in the *luxury industry*, the maximum percentage is high; comparatively, in the *extractive industry*, it is lower due to commoditized goods)
3.	Calculate the royalty rate—a brand strength index is applied to the royalty range to determine the royalty rate
4.	Determine brand-specific revenues by estimating the proportion of parent company revenues that are attributable to the brand
5.	Determine forecast revenues using a function of historic revenues, equity analyst forecasts, and economic growth rates
6.	Apply the royalty rate to the forecast revenues to derive brand revenues
7.	Define the brand's valuation by discounting brand revenues post-tax to achieve its net present value (NPV)

To conclude, the valuation of a brand is based on its emotional and experiential relationship with its customer and prospect base today combined with its potential for increased brand strength, business growth, and future profitability. The credentials of the seller will be determined by the faith that the buyer has in the bespoke set of criteria that are applied to establish the brand's value-adding characteristics and market power. Once seller and buyer are aligned and endorse the criteria underpinning valuation and the approach and methodology being applied, then the valuation can be calculated, the price negotiated, and the sale transacted.

The defined value of a brand will then, of course, have a direct influence on the future level of investment that a brand owner will be prepared to make in the brand asset, and on the return-on-brand-investment that can be reasonably sought and expected over time.

As a final note, the higher the regard and level of esteem in which the transacting parties are held by the market, as well as the status that the brand is perceived to have in the market, will determine whether or not a successfully executed sale will set a new market benchmark valuation to, in turn, influence the relative values of directly competing or closely comparable alternative brand offers.

Key Takeaways

Valuing a product is one thing (the tangible/functional), valuing a brand is quite another (the intangible/emotional).

Brand valuation is ultimately an accounting exercise that places a defined, explicit monetary value on the economic asset that the brand represents.

The valuation of a brand is based on its emotional and experiential relationship with its existing customer and prospect base, combined with its potential for increased brand strength, business growth, and future profitability.

Seven key factors directly influence the financial value of a brand: unique proposition, brand relevance, competitive position, image strength, market adoption, return-on-brand-investment, and future sales/profit potential.

Brand value calculations are prone to much fluctuation for two overarching reasons: different analytical methodologies produce different brand valuation results and changing market and economic realities at different points in time directly affect financial brand worth.

The Word Wizard	
Expression	**Explanation**
Asset value	The understanding of brands as being business assets and their quantifiable monetary value for inclusion on the company balance sheet
Balanced scorecard	An approach that analyzes strategic measures in addition to traditional financial metrics in order to get a more balanced understanding of brand performance and strength
Brand equity	The commercial value of a brand due to its power in the marketplace as a result of customer preference, loyalty, and goodwill toward the brand
Brand value	The monetary value that can be attributed to a brand's worth at any given point in time due to its market power and appeal
C-suite	C-suite refers to the chief senior executives of an organization. Typically, their titles tend to start with the letter c, such as: chief executive officer (CEO), chief financial officer (CFO), chief operating officer (COO), and chief information officer (CIO)

(continued)

The Word Wizard	
Expression	Explanation
Consumer advocacy	The consumer's commitment to, and public support for, the brand
Goodwill	The positive attitude toward the brand in the market; the extent to which it is held in high regard
Licensor	The person or company that grants a license to another party (a licensee) to enjoy a limited right to use or market a brand
Net Present Value	Net Present Value (NPV) analysis is used to help determine how much an investment, project, or any series of cash flows is worth. NPV is the value of all future cash flows (positive and negative) over the entire life of an investment discounted to the present
Performance-driving asset	A specific feature or attribute that is owned by a business that will distinctly increase the performance and profitability of the business in the market
Psychographic analysis	Analysis of consumer lifestyles via a qualitative methodology used to describe consumers on selected psychological attributes—typically applied to the study of personality, values, opinions, attitudes, interests, and lifestyles
Royalty rate	A payment made by one party, the Licensee, to another party, the Licensor, for the use of the property or intangibles owned by the Licensor. A royalty rate is often expressed as a percentage of the revenues obtained by the Licensee when using the Licensor's property

Experience

When to value a brand?: I have found that most companies instinctively know that their brand has a financial value, but quantifying it remains a far-off horizon where they usually do not need to venture. Their prime attention is focused on leveraging the brand to build reputation and win sales in the immediate, short, and medium term. Brand valuation becomes then the domain of mergers and acquisitions, takeovers and consolidations, buy-ins and buy-outs, and is relegated to a momentary consideration in the course of the longer-term strategic planning of business repositioning, brand extension, and strategic growth.

Expertise

Value the emotional: When thinking about the value of your brand, focus on the emotional connection it has with customers—their emotional takeaway and resulting brand loyalty. That's where the richness and wealth of brand valuation lies; that's what it's all about and what you are seeking to account for.

Example

How to value our brand?: This is one of the most challenging questions that a brand consultant is presented with. It's an easy question to ask, and it's always impressive when a company is thinking this way, as brand value should rightfully be treated as a balance sheet asset. But at the same time, "how do we go about valuing our brand?" is a difficult question to answer. A leading national transport company asked me precisely this question. My response? This is where brand meets accountancy. It's a collaboration of in-company and external expertise in brand, strategy, business analysis, and accountancy, taking a whole-of-company approach to audit and establish specific brand-only earnings and potential. Settling on a preferred, recognized, and reliable methodology to drive the process is key.

CHAPTER 4

Been There, Done That, What Next?

Chapter Overview

Even for those organizations that have already applied brand principles and successfully reaped the rewards, the nature of brand and the pace of market change demand that brand stewardship remains firmly front and center of management priorities. This chapter discusses the rationale for ongoing brand development in the life of an organization; it calls on more companies to become brand-centered; and it emphasizes the vital importance for current exponents of maintaining brand commitment, innovation, and cultural alignment. The forces at work in challenging brand planning today are discussed as is the arrival of a new world order of diversifying social media platforms and integrated, synchronized, personalized brand communication.

Brand Stewardship Is for the Long-Haul Not the Short-Play

Over the last 30 years or so, I have watched branding become recognized, accepted, and understood as both a driver of business success and an asset that has equity and can and should be valued on the company balance sheet. In short, branding has come of age, in the sense that the brand is now understood to represent the very heart and soul of the value proposition that a company, large or small, makes to its target market and end-consumer. So, brand has proven itself in the world of business both as a strategy and a process, and I have been pleased and privileged to journey as a foot soldier and evangelist of brand development en route. Indeed, I have been an activist of, and agitator for, brand-centric change, as brand has gradually come center-stage in marketing planning and business communications.

Brand is now understood to represent the very heart and soul of the value proposition.

Brand has arrived, and not just of course as a business development strategy for the consumer products of global multinationals, but equally for small- and medium-sized enterprises at the national, regional, and local level, be they trading in either the B2C or B2B worlds. In this way, and particularly over the last 20 years, brand has become a universally recognized and accepted marketing philosophy and business discipline; the extent, however, to which it is adequately prioritized and actually implemented in the business and corporate world today still leaves much room for development and improvement. The message is out there, the philosophy is accepted, the evidence of brand-based success is clear, and still, too often, lip service is paid to positioning brand as the driving philosophy of the business; to instigating brand processes for internal activation; and to implementing discernible brand change across systems, people, and communications.

So, while some, if not many, companies and organizations have been on a real brand journey—meaning they've been there and done that!—and have enjoyed the rewards and benefits, both cultural and monetary (in-company and in-market), many have not and are yet to commit in a meaningful and market-impacting manner. On this theme, in *The Customer of the Future: 10 Guiding Principles for Winning Tomorrow's Business* (2019), customer experience futurist Blake Morgan affirms this reality of reluctance when she highlights that while "Employee experience is the first step in creating a customer-focused culture [...] many companies treat culture as an afterthought, particularly in the business-to-business space, where only 14% of large B2B companies have a customer-centric culture." Further, Morgan also maintains elsewhere that "Today many companies are slow to go through a digital transformation which is the first step to becoming more customer-centric." And yet she found that the rewards are great: "Brands that have superior customer experience bring in 5.7 times more revenue than their competitors. Companies that invest in customer experience see financial gains and strong customer-focused cultures" (Morgan, *100 of The Most Customer Centric Companies*, Forbes, June 2019).

The future of business, therefore, must inevitably involve greater, wider commitment of companies to integrating proven brand principles and processes into their organizational plans, systems, and infrastructure; it must inevitably require companies to develop a company ethos that is brand values-led, a company culture that is brand-centric, and a company organization that is designed around mechanizing and delivering the company brand promise and experience.

But that is only taking up the slack!

Because everything is changing! And at quite some pace! Which of course highlights one of the great benefits of branding: that a brand is short-hand in a marketplace swamped with information and white noise. The challenge for branders in this decade and in this generation—and the challenge for getting cut-through with *Generation B* (as defined and discussed in Chapter 1)—is the challenge of succinctness and relevance of message. As articulated in *PR's Goal: 'Talk Less, Say More' as Brevity Becomes Norm* (PR News, May 2014), "…snackable content has become the norm among communicators competing for mindshare. In an increasingly mobile (and hyper-busy) society, the trend in content format has been to serve messages in smaller and smaller morsels that consumers could access without committing much time." The pressure on businesses to be nimble and quick in communication is increasing all the time, and this is exacerbated by two contrasting forces: expansion of media platforms and brevity of message exposure. In short, new digital platforms seem to be cropping up all the time, while people's attention span for reading and internalizing written messages seems to be diminishing in equal measure.

Two contrasting forces: Expansion of media platforms and brevity of message exposure.

In relation to this, as depicted in Figure 4.1, there are a number of market dynamics that are impacting at the macro level on the nature and speed of brand evolution. These are, unsurprisingly, technology-enabled, namely, communication, socialization, personalization, and integration.

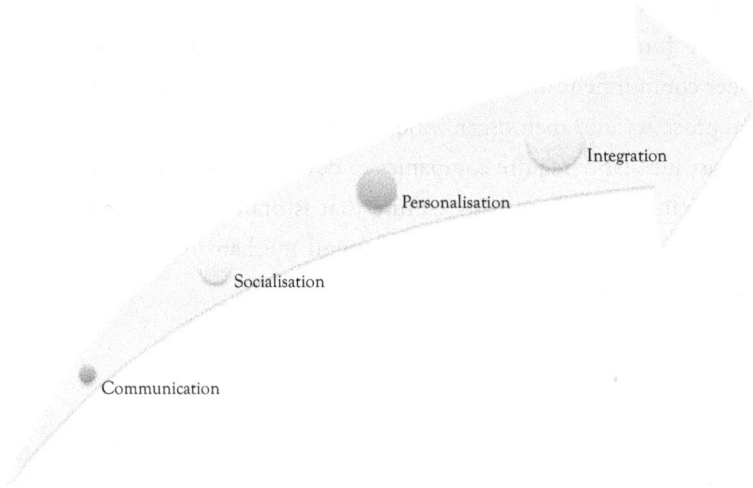

Integration

Personalisation

Socialisation

Communication

Figure 4.1 Technology-enabled macro-level market dynamics

The fact is that the sheer number and churn of communication platforms is constantly on the increase, and it seems exponentially so. Some are *de rigueur* today: Facebook, Snapchat, WhatsApp, Instagram, Twitter, LinkedIn, YouTube. But the landscape changes, and new contenders are inevitable, some replacing existing platforms but others innovating to provide more specific services to specially targeted audiences. Some of these are peer group exclusive (Snapchat is young adults focused), while some are peer group diverse (WhatsApp crosses age groups). This expansion and diversification of social media platforms alone brings both opportunities and threats to brand stewardship: opportunities where brand owners are tuned-in, resourced, and organized to achieve brand presence on new media platforms; threats where they are not. Brands will suffer where they fail to achieve relevant presence in the domain of new media communications, and strong brands, never mind weak ones, need to be aware, analyzing and responding, and keeping up to speed in the full glare of this ongoing market dynamic.

Similarly, the power of online socialization and the omnipresence of online peer groups as facilitated by smartphone and communication apps is an epic dynamic in today's always-on market environment. Brand commitment demands that brand owners and managers must recognize online socialization, understand its relationship and role in achieving or sustaining brand acceptance, and actively channel key brand messages to the relevant set of online social groupings. Brand belief and principles and commitment back at head office are not enough if the impact of peer group socialization and targeted social media messaging receives only lip service or is merely treated with tokenism.

To accentuate further the challenges facing brand strategists today is the development toward, and the inevitable increase in, personalization of brand message and reach. Two management challenges face business owners and leaders here immediately: firstly, how to resource in order to manage the day-to-day social broadcasting of the company's brand messages and to do so with confidence that the tone of voice of the broadcaster is reliably *on-brand* and, secondly, how to analyze/what to make of the exponentially increasing volume of data and information deriving from engaging head-on in this way with the market. A deepening relationship, increasing connectivity, and growing social presence with market intermediaries and the end-consumer are certain to generate much information, feedback, and insights. This brings resource and management challenges, which are sure to increase constantly in line with bespoke personalization of the brand message, market offer, and product or service features to the end-consumer. Again, the point is that having a robust brand strategy and corporate commitment to the brand is one thing; translating that into a personalized and bespoke message and product offer to individual consumers or mini-targeted peer groups is quite another. Digital technology enables this; the future of brand penetration demands this; and cut-through success will depend increasingly on personalization of the message and the offer to individual end-consumers.

While the new world order is one of media diversification and message innovation, with the balance swinging increasingly in favor of social media narrowcasting over traditional media broadcasting, there is at the same time a drive toward integration of brand communications in the market. In *Exploring the Integration of Social Media Within Integrated Marketing Communication Frameworks*, Valos et al. (2016) acknowledged "the rapid growth of SM [Social Media] and their rapid diffusion to organisations" and explained the impetus toward integration in the following terms:

"… the integration of SM provides benefits for organisations, consumers and marketing applications. For organisations, the benefits include: speed, reach, lower cost and recruitment tool. The benefits for consumers include: two-way conversations, WOM [word of mouth] advocacy, value proposition enhancement and younger audience. Marketers could benefit from advocacy leading to new customers, brand awareness, customer service channel, support for above the line campaigns, brand equity, positioning and integrated marketing programs."

In summary, integration is beneficial at two levels: firstly, reverse-integration of social media into a company's in-house digital media program and resource, and, secondly, cross-integration of digital platforms for maximizing message reach and synchronization. The idea of integration of brand communications is that there should be a seamless connection and harmony between the outside world of digitally powered technology and social platforms and the in-company world of brand marketing and communications practice. The concept of reverse-integration of digital platforms into the company's communications programming is to, in a sense, bring the market into the boardroom (or at least into the marketing office!). It is about embracing new technologies and appropriate social media applications as they arise and assessing these for relevance and activation within the brand communications and marketing program. This demands having a culture of openness and trust, and curiosity in the new technologies. It also requires having an attitude of creativity, entrepreneurship, and leadership in taking new approaches, testing new possibilities, and innovating for communications effectiveness. In this way, companies and brands will be always in touch, always up to date, and *always-on*.

In contrast, the concept of cross-integration between media platforms is to harmonize and align brand messaging activity across all the company's active media channels. The principle here is to both unify and synchronize the communication of messages into the market for brand impact and maximum market reach. Brand impact is achieved by the market receiving brand messages in one synchronized communication. This will include both generic and bespoke messaging as relevant to targeted sectors, peer groups, and individual consumers. Market reach is maximized by utilizing all the existing social communication channels at the disposal of the company. This avails of the target audience databases of each channel to ensure that all relevant market contacts are included and engaged in concerted and consistent company and brand communications.

Key Takeaways

Brand cut-through in the market depends increasingly on succinctness and personalization of the brand message and offer to individual consumers.

Two contrasting forces are exacerbating business pressure: expansion of media platforms on the one hand and brevity of message exposure on the other.

The power of online socialization and the omnipresence of online peer groups is an epic dynamic in today's always-on market environment.

Two key management challenges today: how to resource social broadcasting and tone of voice management, and how to analyze the exponentially increasing volume of market information.

Reverse-integration of digital platforms into the company's communications programming brings the market into the boardroom.

Cross-integration between media platforms harmonizes brand messaging activity across all the company's active media channels.

The Word Wizard	
Expression	**Explanation**
B2B	Business-to-business
B2C	Business-to-consumer
Cross-integration	The inter-connection of different communication platforms to achieve enhanced coordination and market impact
Macro level	High-level marketwide strategic concepts, developments, or trends
Market segment	A specific category of customers within the market who have comparable needs and demands—they possess identical or similar requirements, expectations, or desires

(continued)

The Word Wizard	
Expression	**Explanation**
Marketing philosophy	The accepted understanding of the strategic place and power of marketing, and its component systems and tools, in achieving and sustaining successful business development
Niche market	A relatively confined, select, or specialist customer grouping or sector of the market
Online socialization	The act and community-building effect of messaging and socializing via digital platforms
Reverse-integration	The establishment of a systems connection and an open channel of communication between the company and the market, where the company mirrors current marketplace norms of activity and adapts to changing market behavior in real time
Social media narrowcasting	The highly targeted messaging and promotion of a brand via social media platforms to niche market segments, consumer groups, or individuals

Experience

Imitate, innovate, integrate: It has been my experience that even the best of companies can disappear—much to the surprise of market observers and even expert forecasters. No brand can afford to rest on its laurels! Recession can cause it of course: construction companies for example take a drubbing in the course of world or national economic downturns and credit crunches, and likewise, architects and building support service providers. But, changes in consumer behavior can certainly cause it too. At the time of writing, the UK retail high street is suffering in extremis with major branded chains responding belatedly to the growth in online shopping by cutting costs and urgently closing stores. In retrospect, one can wonder and debate just why it took so long for seasoned businesses and established brands to react to what sometimes seem like inevitable, predictable customer trends. Whatever the consensus, one thing's for sure—these market crises show that a big gap can quickly open up between a business and its consumer. A misalignment develops between customer buying behavior and corporate marketing strategy as the speed of brand response fails to keep up with the pace of market change. Things get out-of-kilter! *Imitation* of agile corporate responders, their insights, and winning formulae is an immediate but minimum response; plus, *innovation* is necessary to regain the profitable market high-ground; and *(re)integration* of the company and its brands with volatile consumer demands is essential to realign and rebuild market position, brand image, and customer loyalty. Keeping close to the customer has always been a central tenet of marketing philosophy. Yet, even the best branded companies can appear to forget this hallowed principle and be caught off-guard by dynamic market change, many even disappearing altogether from our business and retail landscape. Whatever happened to Kodak.....? Woolworths…? Blockbuster….? ….

Expertise
Substantiate your brand: Many companies need to be much clearer about their brand message, their target customer, and their communication channels. Branding is otherwise only visual window-dressing, lacking the substance that good customer research and strategic planning brings—which is essential to ensure a great match between what the brand is offering and what the consumer is looking for.

Expertise
Branding never stops: Branding is never done—the world is changing too fast for that.

Expertise
Brands communicate: Brands tell a story that is faithful to the corporate vision and mission, and must continue to do so in a fast-changing media marketplace. This is not about identity design, it's about integrating values, innovation, and communications to gain and maintain stand-out and to make a difference that counts and is recognized.

Example
Integrate for effectiveness not efficiencies: An international airport client engaged me to set up and lead a national marketing communications team straddling traditional and social media programs. The goal: to develop brand position and passenger count in a European national market. The diversity in this work was as refreshing as the strands of

activity were challenging. Creativity of marketing message, relevance of communication channels, and consistency of *brand voice* were paramount. All was delegated to me/my team to plan, execute, and implement … and to good effect. We got results fast, and not only in media listenership, viewership, and engagement but also in customer footfall and annual sales. In a word, success! And we were proudly and publicly attributed with same by the client. Then what? That which was delegated gradually became integrated—success bred broader stakeholder attention, which in equal measure bred a desire for taking more internal control. Our work on social media messaging and blogging for example was taken in-house and integrated into systems and programs run by internal marketing resources. Maybe not completely surprising you might say, but the messaging became generic, the local market culture was ignored, and the brand voice was lost. Integration yes, but localization no; efficiencies maybe but effectiveness definitely not!

Example
Don't over-expect and under-invest: One client of mine in the chemicals manufacturing sector talks with pride about how he has successfully pivoted his business around a newly defined brand strategy, which has led to a sea-change in the organization, its systems, and of course, its branding. For this CEO, the process is never-ending as his customer needs evolve, his communication channels change, and his company competences morph and increase. For another, in international distribution, it was a case of invest in brand presentation to win short-term new business. Two successful investments, but the latter will never deliver the goals of the former. And that's okay as long as you know it. Know your goal and then don't over-expect and under-invest.

CHAPTER 5

The 9:6:3 Guide to Brand Growth

Chapter Overview

Branding means different things to different folks and is made up of many moving parts. Ultimately, the talk and thinking around branding will lead to a focus on brand leadership, and the principles, truths, and challenges that influence the achievement of brand growth. This chapter defines, details, and describes key considerations here and recommends to the reader governing guidelines for the journey to brand success.

The Principles, Truths, and Challenges of Brand Leadership

There is so much talk in business circles about brands and branding, and invariably, this takes place in the context of discussions about market trends, customer demands, and commercial competitiveness. The subject is huge because there is a diverse if not daunting array of places to focus, points to discuss, and perspectives to take when the brand word is mentioned. Some commentators default to strategy, even more to design and a few to employee branding or internalization. Everyone talks about awareness as if this alone was the Holy Grail when in fact it is far from it, as I explain elsewhere. So, the branding conversation can be circuitous and convoluted. Different folks will have different priorities, personal experiences, and beliefs about the underlying principles, truths, and challenges of achieving brand leadership and brand growth. Having a few decades of experience under my belt on brand-building, I thought, therefore, I would join in the debate to add a voice of experience from an external, expert advisor perspective while hopefully contributing to conventional wisdom and even providing some direction or new thinking. So, here you have it, my distillation of all brand knowledge (well, of mine at least!) in a summary shorthand guide, which I have called the *9:6:3 Guide to Brand Growth*: 9 principles of brand success, 6 brand truths, 3 brand challenges. Here goes:

9 Brand Principles:

- Be true to you: your uniqueness
- Inside–outside brand alignment
- Watch your brand space
- Tone, texture, touch, taste
- Mind your language; mind your look
- Consistency drives credibility
- Surprise yourself: whatever you do, stand out
- Hone your brand process
- Lead from the front: brand belief is a leadership imperative

6 Brand Truths:

- Experience trumps product and service … every time
- Value does not mean cheap
- Brand culture is the Holy Grail
- Employees live brands
- Customers love brands
- Brands evolve … always

3 Brand Challenges:

- Be different: invent something!
- Be informed: research, interrogate, integrate
- Be resourced: partner with the best brand talent

Now to expand on each of the preceding principles, truths, and challenges, let's take them one at a time to explore their rationale:

Be True To You: Your Uniqueness

Brands can often be accused of amounting only to eye candy or, more harshly, of merely pulling the wool over people's eyes. Generally speaking nothing could be further from the truth. Brands do justice to the blood, sweat, and tears of the employee and talent base of the company who toil day and often night to add value to people's lives through manufacturing and delivering a unique offer and proposition to the customer. Uniqueness is the key: some of that uniqueness is derived from innovative product or service design, and some from the people employed, their values, personality, behaviors, and organizational culture.

> *Brands do justice to the blood, sweat, and tears of the*
> *employee and talent base of the company.*

Brand is not a sticking plaster to aid business recovery or success; brand is the very essence and uniqueness of the organization, its product, and, crucially, its people—it is what the company and its people are uniquely great at and famous for, or what they deserve to be famous for. Mimicry is the enemy; never be tempted to copycat. Companies must be true to themselves and to their particular uniqueness, be that in their tangible or intangible features, characteristics, systems, or inherent philosophy and values. It is this that gives sustainable stand-out and distinctive competitive position in the market; it is this that has resonance and credibility and unique commercial appeal with the customer.

Inside-Outside Brand Alignment

Brands are powerful when their proposition is emphatically experienced both inside and outside the organization in a concerted, coordinated, and consistent delivery and communication. When aligned in this way, where employees believe, endorse, reinforce, and are able to relate to the external brand marketing messages, then the scene is set for great credibility and sustainability of the brand's competitive position into the future. The employee and customer should be *as one* in their understanding, expectation and advocacy of the uniqueness and relevance of the brand offer.

Watch Your Brand Space

Once you've won your brand space in the market, then you need to defend it. The more successful your brand is, the more attention it will receive, and the more the competition will circle. The point is that gaining a foothold or a position in a market is not the end of the brand endeavor, but the beginning. Do not feel that you have accomplished brand success and so sit back on your laurels; competition is inevitable, and watching your brand space becomes a management imperative. In short, putting your brand on the market is one thing, sustaining that position is quite another. Watch and protect your brand space!

Tone, Texture, Touch, Taste

Having defined brand values and a unique brand proposition, and having expressed these in powerful words and graphic images (the two essential ingredients of all branding), does not mean *job done*! Far from it!—brand consumption is always a *felt* experience: it is powerfully shaped by emotional attributes in a nuanced interaction between brand and consumer. Subtlety and sophistication in its consumption are powerful in the customer's engagement and formative of the customer's perception; this is residual and memorable by nature, and early user or consumer impressions are inevitably evoked later at future point-of-purchase or consumption. In this context, following brand launch, an ongoing prerequisite is to monitor, understand, and micro-manage the subtleties of brand tone of voice, the communication of personality characteristics, and the consistency of the consumption experiences of texture, taste, and touch—not just the visual look, therefore, but the tactile feel and experience of the brand. Micro-management of the brand across these attributes for reliability of its delivered sensual experience is of paramount importance in shaping and sustaining customer perceptions, expectations, and ongoing brand reputation.

Mind Your Language; Mind Your Look

Paying attention to how a brand communicates both visually and aurally is fundamental to brand practice and ongoing brand guardianship. The formally prepared and documented *brand identity guidelines* are your friend here; these should provide good and essential counsel in the do's and don'ts of brand identity management and standards, for the protection of disciplined visual consistency across all markets, sectors, departments, functions—including (crucially) internal and external creative resources and agencies. Nevertheless—and definitely where identity guidelines are not prepared or not implemented—inconsistencies do evolve over time and between geographies and business functions. *Mind your language, mind your look* might seem like a basic principle and basic advice—and it is!—but poor discipline, guardianship, and a lack of a sense of ownership is, in my experience, too common too often; it speaks volumes, and negatively so of course, to internal and external audiences, employees, partners, and stakeholders about the commitment and priorities of the company and the state of health of its brand vision, strategy, and values. Alternatively, diligent attention to detail and good discipline in the brand's use of language, messaging, and design will clearly demonstrate a brand-centric organization. This will reflect belief in the brand and dedication to its market position as well as care and respect for its stakeholders and customers. It is they who are, after all, being asked to accept and buy into the company's brand as a credible, consistent, and cohesive commercial offer. Fastidious and professional discipline in the messaging and look of the brand's presentation is a minimum to be expected and a mandatory to be provided.

Consistency Drives Credibility

People like consistency. They like to know what to expect and to feel confident that they will get the same experience every time they purchase and consume a product. A brand promises this. It promises not only uniqueness of experience but also reliability in its purchase, use, consumption, and value add. A brand promises consistency. And consistency denotes planning, insight, customer knowledge, and professional, effective management skills. It demonstrates that the company or brand owner has pride in the brand, a standard to hit, a target experience to deliver, and a vision for what the product or service is to achieve and how that is to be different from competing offers.

Consistency—the repeated, reliable promise and delivery of a known standard of customer experience and satisfaction—demonstrates that the seller understands the buyer, and that buyers feel that the product is designed and delivered for them personally, in accordance with their specific needs and preferences. Every time. This nurtures a relationship of deep trust between seller and buyer, which constitutes a brand relationship: customers know and understand the value transaction that is on offer, they appreciate the relevance of the brand to their lives, and they integrate the product into their lives, which builds belief and great credibility in the brand. And credibility is infectious in the market as word spreads, which is of course great for business.

Surprise Yourself: Whatever You Do, Stand Out

The element of surprise is good to have in business as it is in battle. And it takes a little courage and lots of creativity—so be brave: surprise yourself and everyone else in the market by standing out, by being different, by not being the same! And the place to start is with yourself: if you're not surprising yourself, you're probably surprising no one else either. This means surprise yourself by not settling for the ordinary, the mundane, the monotonous, the expected when choosing and using words and images around your business and your brand. It's just not good enough to be as good as everyone else! That means you're just the same as everyone else! Imitation may, as the saying goes, be the sincerest form of flattery, but it is the weakest form of branding—in fact it's not branding at all. Why? Because it doesn't achieve stand-out, it doesn't surprise anyone, it makes you and your brands look, feel, and be the same as all the rest. There's no point in being the same, no point at all! Sameness makes you a commodity and therefore easily replaced or competed with.

It's just not good enough to be as good as everyone else!

A core brand principle is to *stand out*: be different, even unique, and thereby easily seen, fully appreciated, and quickly preferred. A similar (but different!) core brand principle is to *be outstanding*: deliver differential excellence that beats competing offers and is a distinctly better buy for the target customer. Standing out when you're outstanding is just fair play— an outstanding brand deserves to stand out!! It deserves to be seen, to be talked about, to be promoted, and to communicate its best-in-class better offer and superb value to the marketplace. So, whatever you do, stand out!!

Hone Your Brand Process

Little or nothing stays the same or remains fixed for long in markets, business, or indeed the customer's life, so, likewise, branding and the brand process should be constantly reviewed, updated, and refreshed to keep the customer in full focus and the relevance of the brand resonating resolutely at all times. Things change and so should your brand process, as you constantly work to achieve an ever closer and deeper relationship between the product or service produced, the market channels and the final customer or consumer experience.

A brand process should be refocused or recalibrated over time to evolve with the customer and to take account of market changes and dynamics that affect the relevance of your brand and its uniqueness and reception in the market. A key principle here is to prioritize market research and intelligence relating to brand positioning and performance and to ensure to have a system or process of continuously listening to customers. The insights deriving from this process must activate incremental changes and developments over time in product or service design, brand messaging and visual expression in order to respond to customer requirements, competitive threats, and any impacting macro-level market movements and dynamics.

To hone a brand process, you need to have a brand process in the first place, and one which encompasses market research, brand strategy, communications planning, and creative execution. Honing the brand process then accepts that change happens—and usually all the time—and often exponentially so. It seeks to keep the process of customer–company communication and creativity aligned so that brand impact and effectiveness can be maintained and managed for maximum added value, market performance, and customer experience. Honing your brand process is about committing to continuous analysis, planning, and refocusing of the brand experience to ensure the brand moves with the times, reflects new customer insights, repositions for competitive strength, and protects the company from relying on legacy thinking, out-of-date strategies, or increasingly ineffectual creativity.

Lead From the Front: Brand Belief Is a Leadership Imperative

Brand is always a strategic matter in any company, and brand investments are invariably decided at the boardroom table. Auditing or researching a brand must always include the CEO and the company leadership team so that the brand owners can have their say, will comprehensively buy into the process, will understand the importance and rationale of the project—and will be (and feel) included and excited about the imminent brand goals and outcomes. This is because brand strategy impacts on the very image and destiny of a company and can and should (and must!) direct the proposition and values of the company, its products, and people into the future.

Given, therefore, the fundamental nature of brand as a determinator of the future experience and relevance of the company, it is critical that there is real belief in the brand, and that this belief is ascribed to, and championed by, the CEO and the senior management team. In short, brand belief is a leadership imperative without which the company will be seen to be paying lip service to brand philosophy and scant regard to brand strategy.

Furthermore, as a values-based endeavor, it is vital that the company brand is expressed and explained right across the employee base and that people internalize the brand values and bring these to life through brand-based behaviors and actions. A unified brand-centric organization—whose people understand and authentically implement the brand values—is a powerful statement to the market and an essential condition for making a confident brand promise. To effect and sustain such a change in behavior—and often a change in the very culture of the organization itself—the CEO and the leadership team need to lead from the front and demonstrate their belief in the brand, its purpose, its values, and its proposition. Anything less than a wholly unified pan-company approach will hamper brand credibility outside, will disable brand engagement inside, and will create confusion generally, including in the market. It is imperative, therefore, that company leadership commits to the brand change, publicly demonstrates brand belief, and leads by example inside and outside the organization.

Experience Trumps Product and Service.... Every Time

Experience is a great word in branding—much better than values or positioning or identity or digital because it implies greatness and innovation and just nails the very purpose and end-goal of having a brand in the first place. A brand must do justice to a company's differential proposition and capability by making sure that such uniqueness is experienced in the market so that customers can recognize it, relate to it, and buy it. In this transaction, customers should and must be given a great experience every time—they should be left with the memory of an emotional experience, not just product benefits, which they see as at least different and hopefully outstanding. I believe that what makes a brand great has so often so little to do with the actual product or service elements provided. It's *the experience* that engages customers and consumers ... that converts their decision to buy into a decision to buy again and again. To think, therefore, of branding as being experiential in nature is to elevate a product or service to a higher plane of possibility and market impact. This is where product features and service components are valued not just for their physical attributes or direct user benefits but also collectively for their psychological and emotional impact on consumers and their sense of self-esteem and personal prestige.

> *What makes a brand great has so often so little to do with*
> *the actual product or service elements provided.*

Ultimately, and necessarily, through insightful strategic brand marketing, products and services are able to offer and deliver emotional experiences to consumers, which the intrinsic physical elements or ingredients on their own cannot. As I say, *"75 percent of what makes a brand great has nothing to do with the product or service delivered!"*—but it has lots to do with the emotion, personality, and tone of voice of brand behavior, messaging, and imagery, and related to this, peer group identification and adoption. Because of this emotional outcome and its powerful influence on customer perception, recall, and loyalty, experience absolutely trumps product and service—and does indeed do so every time.

Value Does Not Mean Cheap

I know we know this as a truth—at least in the emotional right side of our brains we do—but yet I believe it warrants being said again and again, so here it is again: value does not mean cheap! And often it means blimmin expensive! Recently, I visited a very high-class restaurant (I was brought as a guest!), and inevitably, I was asked by a friend afterward what I thought of it: *Twice the price of most other leading restaurants but three times the value!* I said. *I'll be back!* That's value for you—it brings you back, and it does so never mind the cost because you know you're getting more for your money. So, a *value product*, a *value offer*, a *value deal* better mean that you're getting more for your money, else it's not value at all, it's just plain cheap. And cheap by definition means poor quality, albeit at a low price. We've all heard the saying "you get what you pay for," and while this may be more generalization than fact, it does carry more than a modicum of truth. And then again, value is in the experience of the buyer just as beauty is in the eye of the beholder. What I mean here is that different buyers experience different purchases in different ways. Some do so more emotionally than others, having strong natural bonds of affinity with a particular brand of product or service, which in turn generates specific brand loyalty.

> *Value is in the experience of the buyer just as beauty is in the eye of the beholder.*

Some folks therefore are not just buying product ingredients or features—indeed, as I hope you'll agree, most aren't. Whether they recognize it or not, or even admit it or not, most people make a branded purchase for underlying and often deep-seated, emotional reasons way beyond the specific functionality of the item itself. So, value is attributed—and significantly so—from the emotional reward that is enjoyed by the buyer or consumer as well as from the functional satisfaction or benefit that is derived. The full value of a purchase must be seen not only in quantitative terms but also in emotional, self-esteem, and peer group identity gains that brands so wonderfully provide, be that at a high price or low.

Brand Culture Is the Holy Grail

When all is said and done, the word *culture* comes into play: it is the ultimate ambition of a brand-led company. In the brand world, there is much talk about values, propositions, emotions, positioning, design, creativity, digital, consumer profiles, communications, brand engagement, and so on. When this is all wrapped up and looked at in the round, what we are seeking and what we are left with is a brand culture—or at least that should be the strategic intent. Culture is the foundation, driver, and sustainer of brand experience. It is what you get when you develop a business around a set of specific values and principles, and when you organize your business to nurture, deliver, communicate, and live those inside and out. As such, culture—along with brand experience—is the Holy Grail because it can only be achieved and sustained by disciplined and consistent commitment to the cherished beliefs of the organization and its underlying and expressed motives. When the company is consistently, reliably, and publicly living by its values and beliefs, then it has developed a culture; it will be recognized and rewarded for this by the brand loyalty not only of the marketplace but also of the employee base.

Employees Live Brands

Employees are the first line of defense and of delivery of the company brand (corporate or product level). Their awareness, understanding, and behavior around the brand speak volumes to the market about whether the company walks the brand walk as well as talks the brand talk. If the brand is meaningful at all (which any true brand must be!), then it has to resonate with its first-line custodians and believers—its handlers: employees. Employees congregate every day to produce, support, implement, communicate, and sell the brand and in the case of many famous international brands (Apple, Dell, Google, Mercedes, McDonalds, etc.) it can be said that employees work for the brand and not just for the company, and certainly not just for the inherent (technical) product or service. In this way, employees live brands and must always do so if a meaningful, relevant, value-adding relationship is not only to be established and developed but also sustained in the market. The employee has an intimate relationship with the brand in servicing the brand's production, distribution, protection, and communication needs; the employee has a vital responsibility in advocating and advising customers on the brand's points of difference, unique features, benefits, and emotional equity. It is axiomatic that employees are central to a brand's credibility and consistency in delivery, and it is imperative, therefore, that the brand's values become internalized by employees and integrated into their psyche, with the brand, ideally, being adopted into their own purchase, usage, and consumption repertoire. Employees must at least live brands; customers, however, must love brands.

Customers Love Brands

With customers it's love! It's emotional: the brand should bring something different, special, unique that customers recognize, cherish, and integrate into their lives. Logically, this could be merely a (low) price-based offer, but if so, its availability and quality point (*value*) have got to sustain as it is unlikely to bring any other differentiation, peer group applause, or self-esteem benefits! And yes, of course, there are bargains to be had, but a snatch and grab bargain is unlikely to be the start of a beautiful and ongoing brand relationship! On the contrary, a brand *relationship* is sustained by emotional reward (not just by a tangible, rational transaction), which makes the customer feel good, understood, discerning, affirmed.

> *A snatch and grab bargain is unlikely to be the start of a beautiful and ongoing brand relationship!*

Customers love brands because of the emotional takeaway they enjoy from the purchase and consumption at a psychological, perceptual, and personal level. Overall, a brand's added value can be defined in terms of functionality (usage), image (external), and self-esteem (internal): the customers' value experience, therefore, includes how the brand makes them feel, how they are seen, and how they see themselves. In short, a good brand affects a person's life and can be life-changing; customers love the effect it has on them, both functionally and emotionally, and very especially how it makes them feel.

Brands Evolve ... Always

Some branding practitioners make a big play of emphasizing that a brand (its values), once defined, never changes ... ever! I'm not so adamant. I do agree of course that tactical use of brand messaging and imagery may wander with the winds of market change but that core brand values should *in principle* remain set, constant, and committed to. And there lies the rub, because even here, thinking about a company's brand values, innate and endemic as they are, is there not ever some room for maneuver, for parsing, for taking a fresh look? I think there is—even with the brand values. The reason I say so is that, although brand values are generally and rightly regarded as sacred, the process of their definition is, in itself, not so much a science as an art. Yes, the process requires erudite investigation, intelligent insights, and distillation of brand truths, differences, and nuances, and yet quantitative analysis gets us only so far (and not far enough!) in the irrefutable resolution of a brand's attributes, characteristics, and values. Why? Because brand definition is essentially both a root-and-branch process of exploration and a collective consensus that is qualitatively based. This being so, empirical analysis must ultimately and necessarily be complemented with, and overlaid by, expert intuition, marketing instinct, and innovative cross-referencing of qualitative consumer insights and brand information. I guess, therefore, I am of a school of thinking that would recommend you hold your values high but scrutinize them carefully and often.

As sacrosanct as they are, in the face of business disruption and market dynamics, it is judicious to run the rule over a company's underlying and governing business directives (such as its brand values) as the business changes, becomes more experienced, and adopts or strives for new cultural characteristics, expressions, and norms. In short, pay attention to your values in times of change and don't ignore them or take them for granted just because they're already defined. Review them for fresh interpretation, meaning, and implications. Always be quick to evolve their communication and messaging into the market for alignment with changing consumer needs, experiences, and expectations. To remain ever-relevant, always evolve your brand.

Be Different: Invent Something!

Why be the same as everyone else or, indeed, anyone else? And yet, it seems to be inherent to our human psyche that we should fit in with the crowd and look and behave the same as our peers, be that our social or our business peers. It's as if, instinctively, we are in an interminable state of pubescent angst about standing out! And, in my experience, this applies and manifests itself so often in business. Just looking *over the shoulder* in business to check how we compare with our business peers or competitors is not, you will agree, a recipe for smart and sustainable business success, right? So, how to break the duck? How to beat the posse? How to take center stage? How to get the limelight?

> *We are in an interminable state of pubescent*
> *angst about standing out!*

The answer, of course, is clear: see what the others are doing, saying, showing ... and then do something different! But that takes courage, it takes inventiveness, it takes confidence in your read and understanding of the bounds of possibility, the scope of strategic stretch, and the latitude of lateral thinking. It takes guts, and it takes creative guts! The temptation to *fit in* with the sector, its exponents, players, and commentators is probably the number one reason why many companies—be they large- and medium-sized enterprises (LMEs) or small- and medium-sized enterprises (SMEs)—seem to pay scant regard to branding, to defining and investing in their values, to championing and communicating a unique brand proposition. On the contrary, *difference* is the dynamo that energizes competitive positioning. Being different—while always being true to your values—is the only sane philosophy to hold to in an open, free-market economy if the brand is to have any worthwhile chance, meaning, or relevance with consumers or if it is to garner any financially leverageable and sustainable position in the market. The commercial risk, of course, is there, but then the prize is usually high. Anyway, sometimes, a company has no choice in the matter where, over time, sameness, commoditization, and loss of advantage has eroded profitability, necessitating a rethink, a refocus, and a repositioning for resonance and relevance across the marketwide target audience base.

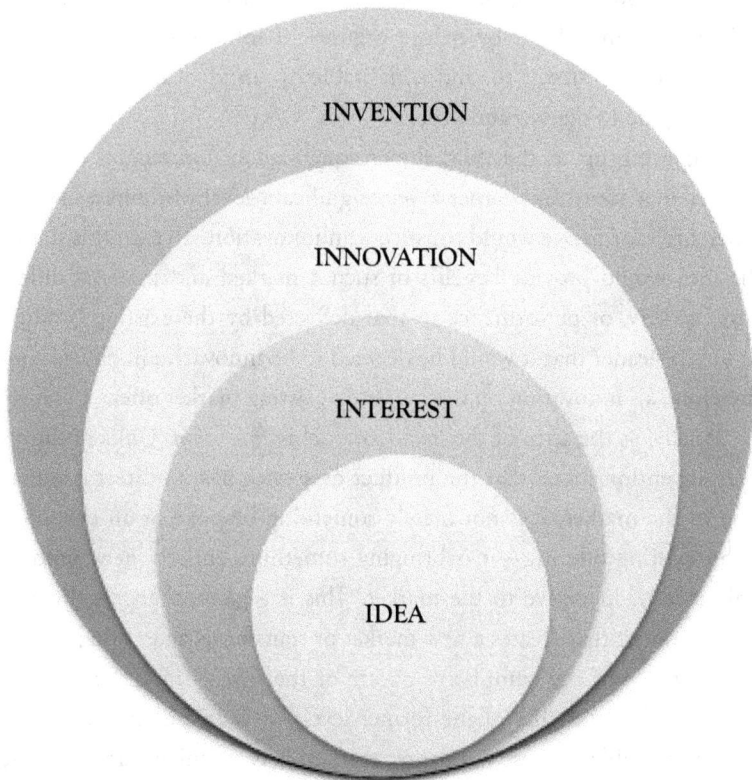

Figure 5.1 The four I's of brand potential

"Difference" is the dynamo that energizes competitive positioning

Of course, there are naturally varying levels of difference that can be sought and achieved in the brand's market. I express this in Figure 5.1 where I have coined *The four I's of brand potential,* namely idea, interest, innovation, invention. These four levels are cumulative in potential and value, working up as they do from a mere idea to a validated and verified, marketable invention. The purpose of this thought is to simply set out a series of four comparative levels of visioning that a company, marketer, or brander can hold or strive for in seeking to transform the company or the brand:

Idea is the fundamental floor for all change, meaning that one must have an original idea that is different, novel, or innately attractive. Secondly, and building on the latter, *Interest* demands that the idea, although technically or by nature original in some way, is of tangible (or emotional) interest to, and is desirable by, an identifiable consumer demographic or market audience.

Migrating up to the third dimension, namely *Innovation*, this recognizes that ideas that garner a very significant level of interest and are inherently distinctive would constitute an innovation. To earn this status, the idea would provide benefits of such a marked and material difference, quality, or performance to that delivered by the existing product or service-leader that it would be deemed to be innovative in nature and, therefore, an innovation on the currently existing market offer.

Finally, at the apex of the *four I's* model is *Invention.* Unlike innovation, invention infers that the product or service has no direct comparison in the market, it is not merely something bespoke or an evolution of an existing offering—it is bringing something entirely new, unique, unknown ... inventive to the market. This is a game-changer; this is a pivot-product that creates a new market or transforms an existing one.

By virtue of the cumulative nature of the *four I's* model, invention possesses all the merits of the former levels: it is an original idea; it is of demonstrable interest to a target market; it is an enhancement of the customer's experience through its quality benefits or performance attributes; it is something new, unique, and relevant in the market. Invention, therefore, constitutes the highest form of creativity and promises the greatest degree of differential for brand relevance, stand-out, and commercial power. It takes the greatest level of creative thinking, ingenuity, commitment, and investment, and it requires vision, passion, and courage to deliver it. If you want to really be different, to really stand out, then invent something—be an inventor! Failing that, you may, at the very least, become an innovator—which I suspect is very good for business too, and for the business' brand!

Be Informed: Research, Interrogate, Integrate

Hunch is great, gut instinct is tantalizing and *knowing which way the wind is blowing* shows confidence in the unquantifiable—and in oneself! All good? Maybe not. Hunch, gut, and dare I say it, wind, can constitute, on the one hand, the deepest understanding or, on the other, the greatest folly. Knowing something is not necessarily the same as being informed, and being informed is not necessarily the same as knowing something. There is a place for both information and intuition in brand decision making—the trick is to get them in the right order and, for my money, it's information first, intuition second.

> *Knowing something is not necessarily the same as being*
> *informed, and being informed is not necessarily*
> *the same as knowing something.*

The challenge, indeed, for many executives and brand owners today is to be in a position to draw more on one's collective intuition and less so just on received empirical data—therefore to translate the learnings from the information into expertly interpreted and intuitively endorsed insights and actions. This is the best of both worlds—the empirical meets the emotional, the informational meets the instinctive, the comprehensible meets the creative, left brain meets right brain! In this way, we engage all our brains, all our executive instincts, all our creative juices and entrepreneurial flair; we bring a multiplier effect to branding decisions that raises eyebrows, gets talked about, and generates stand-out, wreaking havoc sometimes with traditional norms of business practice, existing means of creative expression, and conforming modes of company behavior. So, both are good. But it starts with insightful information.

It may ring of the obvious to say it, but being informed is the basic building block for insightful and intuitive decision making, and surprisingly, therefore, the brand research budget is often insufficient, paltry even, and sometimes, nonexistent. Believe this: research is fundamental to building and sustaining a strong brand. Listening to the target audience in quantitative and qualitative research methodologies is illuminating, insightful, and from the brand's perspective, enriching and essential. It informs the planning and evolution of the customer's experience of the brand, which leads naturally to an increase in customer relevance and engagement—when lessons learned and insights gleaned are implemented for brand relevance. To achieve this outcome, however, demands deep interrogation of the research findings while keeping the target customer or consumer profile wholly front of mind. This customer is the entire *raison d'etre* for the research program in the first place and regular research designs, research panels, and omnibus surveys, and their program managers must always keep this fully in mind. The point is that interrogating research findings for key customer and consumer insights must be a priority activity for brand executives, managers, directors, owners. Moreover, these insights need to be understood and tangibly integrated through product and service innovation, visual design, brand messaging, and market communication. In this way, enhanced, evolved, or bespoke brand benefits will be experienced, and a competitive repositioning of the brand in its market space can take place and be profitably sustained.

Be Resourced: Partner With the Best Brand Talent

You will have heard many leaders, not only in business but in international politics, the voluntary sector and in many other professions, admit that while they may not personally possess the strongest marketing skills or the greatest business nous, they do work hard to gather around themselves those who are more skilled, more expert, more knowledgeable, more connected. In short, they recruit and partner with the best, and it is this, they admit, that drives their personal success. A lesson for all of us! The best people, of course, can reside within an organization, but, equally, they often reside outside it. And this is how business advisors, consultancies, and communications agencies—including brand agencies!—prosper.

Their very prosperity is founded on the basis that the client needs to reach outside itself to seek expert assistance, acquire proprietary process, and engage specific market-relevant capabilities and competences. To enjoy the benefits of the best brand skills, it is imperative to look to where these resources are most readily available and, for this, one must surely look to the best (not the biggest!) brand agencies. To be the best, partner with the best—anything less is to detract from the potential to out-think, out-communicate, out-maneuver, and out-compete the competition; anything less will mean meeting head-on avoidable market barriers and brand challenges, or at least meeting them earlier than otherwise would be prudent or anticipated.

In reaching the end of this book on branding, it is, I believe, a worthy point to make that a company or organization should not be reticent about reaching out to the best brand talent in its business orbit, should not be myopic when it comes to bringing in the best ideas, and should not be short-termist in its thinking about the role and purpose of branding in engendering market and business success. The best brand talent, frequently sourced from outside the organization in the form of brand and communication agencies, should be engaged to help leverage the maximum future success from the innate brand potential of the organization. It should not just be engaged for the purpose of short-term sales success but should be invested in for longer-term brand positioning in the market. It should be commissioned to create or consolidate distinctive market leadership, emotional customer relationship, and sustainable brand experience. Being well-resourced by recruiting and engaging the best brand talent is a key strategy to accelerate market success by building outstanding brand power and thereby stimulating and sustaining sales growth.

Key Takeaways

Brand is not a sticking plaster to aid business recovery or success; brand is the very essence and uniqueness of the organization, its product, and its people.

The employee and the customer should be *as one* in their understanding, expectation, and advocacy of the uniqueness and relevance of the brand offer.

Diligent attention to detail and good discipline in the brand's use of language, messaging, and design will clearly demonstrate a brand-centric organization.

Brand consistency is the repeated, reliable promise and delivery of a known standard of customer experience and satisfaction.

To think of branding as being experiential in nature is to elevate a product or service to a higher plane of possibility and market impact.

Culture is the foundation, driver, and sustainer of brand experience. It is what you get when you develop a business around a set of specific values and principles.

Employees must live brands if a meaningful, relevant, value-adding relationship is not just to be developed but sustained in the market.

Customers love brands because of the emotional takeaway they enjoy from the purchase and consumption at a psychological, perceptual, and personal level.

Invention constitutes the highest form of brand creativity: it is an original idea; it is of demonstrable interest to a target market; it is an enhancement of the customer's experience; it is something new, unique, and relevant in the market.

There is a place for both information and intuition in brand decision making—the trick is to get them in the right order: information first, intuition second.

A core brand principle is to *stand out*: be different, even unique and thereby easily seen, fully appreciated and quickly preferred.

The Word Wizard	
Expression	**Explanation**
Bonds of affinity	Powerful reasons to be naturally, strongly, and consistently attracted to a brand
Brand culture	The commitment, over time, of people to the brand; the effect and experience that is achieved when a company is consistently, reliably, and publicly living by its brand values and beliefs

The Word Wizard	
Expression	**Explanation**
Brand guardianship	Acting as the guardian of a brand's proposition, values, and tone of voice
Brand philosophy	The accepted understanding of the strategic place and power of a brand in achieving and sustaining successful business development
Collective	The group of company stakeholders and expert advisors that is committed to, and responsible for, the planning, design, promotion, and positioning of a brand
Consumption repertoire	The typical set of goods and services and brands that a customer consumes on a repeated basis
Core brand principles	The essential truths and rules relating to the effective planning and achievement of brand growth and success
Emotional equity	The extent to which the intangible, nonphysical, emotional experience of a brand commands customer preference and ongoing loyalty
Empirical analysis	An analysis based on actual research observation or real-life experience as opposed to theory or logical deduction
Legacy thinking	Knowledge, understanding, and perceptions that hark back to historic or previously accepted opinions, beliefs, or experiences
LMEs	Large and medium-sized enterprises
Multiplier effect	Where a result is magnified due to the combined sharing and cross-fertilization of thinking, information, and expertise
Nuance	A subtle difference in behavior, expression, or interpretation
Nuanced interaction	A sophisticated encounter that is highly subtle in its communication and relationship
Pivot-product	A product invention that sets a whole new performance or service benchmark, creating a step-change in the standard of experience and expectation in the market
Repositioning	The act of updating or changing the meaning and proposition of a brand for enhanced market relevance and competitiveness
SMEs	Small and medium-sized enterprises
Value transaction	The exchange of value—via a monetary transaction—between company and customer, between brand and consumer

Experience

Think bigger and bolder and break the mold: I remember well the birth of a new petrol forecourt brand. The investors wanted to create their own brand identity in the national market. The forecourt shop was a big part of the brand development and investment, and the custom in the industry had been to franchise-in the use of a recognized convenience-retailer brand marque. The business owners were poised to invest personally in building this new enterprise, and in so doing, would at the same time be building the value of the franchisor's store brand. Then it dawned … "Why build someone else's brand, when you can build your own?" I challenged. Eyes widened, hearts beat, and plans were made to break the mold and create one unified brand across the entire forecourt offer. Today, this business is a highly successful international retail convenience and hospitality group.

Expertise

Seek the best talent everywhere: Working on a national brand does not mean only working with national talent. Talent comes in all shapes and sizes (as they say) and of course from all parts and places (as I say)! Talent is talent and is not confined by national boundaries or geography. Why not employ all the right and best talent available to create the best brand possible? Digital connectivity reaches all corners of the globe and provides easy access and communication. Working on creating a new national food cuisine brand, I did just that and joyfully engaged great brand talent from the US, UK and EU (including Ireland) to work on building a world-beating, best-in-class brand offer to put Ireland on the international food tourism map.

Expertise

Live your brand: Brand-led organizations are conscious of their brand principles, truths, and challenges every day. Brand success relies on a collective commitment across the company to understand these, to address these, to be true to these, to live these. Your customer expects no less from you—including that you *live your brand*!

Example

Design serves the brand: A European oil company's Head of Marketing asked me for a set of identity design guidelines to localize their brand for a new national market. "We want one of these for Ireland" he said, brandishing a thick identity guidelines manual; "We need to get the content in here right for Ireland." "You don't need an identity manual" I replied, "you first need a brand strategy to guide your market positioning and local communications! And then go compile your brand identity guidelines manual to be influenced by that". I was commissioned to carry out a brand audit immediately. Design serves the brand, always—it's never the other way around.

Bibliography

Aledin, S.A. 2012. *Teenagers' Purposive Brand Relationships: From Social Filters to Shoulders to Lean on.*

Best Global Brands. 2017. "Interbrand." https://interbrand.com/best-brands/best-global-brands/2017/

Britton, M. 2015. *Youthnation: Building Remarkable Brands in a Youth-Driven Culture*, 1st ed. Hoboken, New Jersey, NJ: John Wiley & Sons.

Bulgarelli, F. June 2015. "Methods of Brand Evaluation." *HEC Paris*, http://docplayer.net/21736168-Methods-of-brand-valuation.html

Coupland, D. 1992. *Generation X: Tales for an Accelerated Culture*. London: Abacus.

Coupland, D. June 1995. *Generation X'd*, Details Magazine, http://coupland.tripod.com/details1.html

Demographic Profile—America's Gen X (PDF). 2013. "MetLife." https://web.archive.org/web/20160817083829/https://metlife.com/assets/cao/mmi/publications/Profiles/mmi-gen-x-demographic-profile.pdf

Dyson, P., A. Farr, and N.S. Hollis. 1996. "Understanding, Measuring, and Using Brand Equity." *Journal of Advertising Research* 36, no. 6, pp. 9–21.

Gershon, R.A. 2017;2016;2015. *Digital Media and Innovation: Management and Design Strategies in Communication.* Los Angeles: Sage.

Global 500. February 2018. "The Annual Report on the World's Most Valuable Brands, Brand Finance." https://brandfinance.com/knowledge-centre/reports/brand-finance-global-500-2018/

Haigh, D. 1999. "Understanding the Financial Value of Brands." http://citeseerx.ist.psu.edu/viewdoc/download?doi=10.1.1.199.8159&rep=rep1&type=pdf

Howe, N. 2014. "How the Millennial Generation is Transforming Employee Benefits." *Benefits Quarterly* 30, no. 2, pp. 8–14.

Howe, N., and S. William. 2000. Millennials Rising: The Next Great Generation.

Hunter, M. 2013. "A Short History of Business and Entrepreneurial Evolution during the 20th Century: Trends for the New Millennium." *Geopolitics, History, and International Relations* 5, no. 1, pp. 44–98.

Jackson, R.L., and M.A. Hogg. *Encyclopedia of Identity*. Thousand Oaks, Calif; London: SAGE Publications.

Kantar, M.B. 2015. "BrandZ Valuation Methodology." http://millwardbrown.com/brandz/rankings-and-reports/top-global-brands/2015/methodology

Kantar, M.B. May 2018. "BrandZ Top 100 Most Valuable Global Brands 2018." http://millwardbrown.com/brandz/rankings-and-reports/top-global-brands/2018

Kapferer, J. 2012. *The New Strategic Brand Management: Advanced Insights and Strategic Thinking*, 5th ed. London, Philadelphia: Kogan Page.

Kompella, K. 2014. *The Definitive Book of Branding*. Los Angeles: Sage.

Landor. May 2016. "Stop The Chest Beating: The End of Monetary Brand Valuation." https://landor.com/thinking/stop-the-chest-beating-the-end-of-monetary-brand-valuation

McCrindle, M. 2014. "The ABC of XYZ: Understanding the Global Generations." (*used by permission of McCrindle Research*). https://academia.edu/35646276/The_ABC_of_XYZ_-_Mark_McCrindle_PDF.pdf

Morgan, B. 2019. "100 of The Most Customer-Centric Companies." *Forbes*. https://forbes.com/sites/blakemorgan/2019/06/30/100-of-the-most-customer-centric-companies/?sh=2b9612e963c3

Morgan, B. 2019. *The Customer of the Future: 10 Guiding Principles for Winning Tomorrow's Business*. HarperCollins Leadership.

Morgan, J. 2014. *The Future of Work: Attract New Talent, Build Better Leaders, and Create a Competitive Organization*, 1st ed. Hoboken, New Jersey, NJ: John Wiley & Sons, Inc.

Mosley, R. 2014. *Employer Brand Management: Practical Lessons from the World's Leading Employers*, 1st ed. Chichester, West Sussex, United Kingdom: Wiley.

Ooma inc. September 16, 2019. "Product Cost Quotations." https://ooma.com/home-phone/cell-phone-cost-comparison/

Owen, M. 2002. *Developing Brands with Qualitative Market Research*, 5. London, Thousand Oaks, CA: Sage.

PR News. May 2014. *PR's Goal: 'Talk Less, Say More' as Brevity Becomes Norm*. Access Intelligence, LLC.

Rocha, M. 2014. "Brand Valuation, A Versatile Strategic Tool for Business." *Interbrand*, https://slideshare.net/digitalmarketingvn/brand-valuation-a-versatile-strategic-tool-for-business

Salinas, G. 2009;2011. *The International Brand Valuation Manual: A Complete Overview and Analysis of Brand Valuation Techniques, Methodologies and Applications*, 1st ed. Chichester, U.K: Wiley.

Stengel, J. 2011. *Grow: How Ideals Power Growth and Profit at the World's 50 Greatest Companies*, 10. New York, NY: Crown Business.

Tybout, A.M., T. Calkins, and Kellogg School of Management. 2019. *Kellogg on Branding in a Hyper-Connected World*, 1st ed. Hoboken, New Jersey, NJ: John Wiley & Sons, Inc.

Valos, M.J., F.H. Habibi, R. Casidy, C.B. Driesener, and V.L. Maplestone. 2016. "Exploring the Integration of Social Media within Integrated Marketing Communication Frameworks: Perspectives of Services Marketers." *Marketing Intelligence and Planning* 34, no. 1, pp. 19–40.

Wind, J., and C.F. Hays. 2016. *Beyond Advertising: Reaching Customers through Every Touchpoint*, 2nd ed. Hoboken: John Wiley & Sons, Incorporated.

Yohn, D.L. 2014. *What Great Brands do: The Seven Brand-Building Principles that Separate the Best from the Rest*, 1st ed. San Francisco, CA: Jossey-Bass, A Wiley Brand.

Word Wizard: Grand Summary

Expression	Explanation
Asset value	The understanding of brands as being business assets and their quantifiable monetary value for inclusion on the company balance sheet
Attributes	Key characteristics, features, or qualities
Balanced scorecard	An approach that analyzes strategic measures in addition to traditional financial metrics in order to get a more balanced understanding of brand performance and strength
B2B	Business-to-business
B2C	Business-to-consumer
Bonds of affinity	Powerful reasons to be naturally, strongly, and consistently attracted to a brand
Brand	Uniqueness you know, want, and trust
Brand associations	The perceptions, experiences, and reputation that people associate with a brand
Brand behaviors	The behavior, activities, and interaction of those responsible for planning, producing, and promoting the brand
Brand believers	Those who believe that a brand is an effective business and profit driver
Brand-centric	The organization of a business around promising and delivering a brand values and culture-based experience to its customer base
Brand champions	Those within the employee base who are instinctively and outstandingly disposed toward, and passionate about, the brand
Brand council	A hand-picked leadership team that takes responsibility for guiding and managing the development, approval, and deployment of a new brand
Brand culture	The commitment, over time, of people to the brand; the effect and experience that is achieved when a company is consistently, reliably, and publicly living by its brand values and beliefs
Brand equity	The commercial value of a brand due to its power in the marketplace as a result of customer preference, loyalty, and goodwill toward the brand
Brand essence	The ultimate thumbprint of the brand's meaning; the distilled (typically three-word) shorthand for what a brand stands for
Brand experience	The full and combined benefits and effect in functional and emotional terms of using or consuming a brand

(continued)

Expression	Explanation
Brand forum	A discussion-based in-company workshop session that deeply explores, investigates, and defines pan-organizational beliefs and perceptions
Brand guardianship	Acting as the guardian of a brand's proposition, values, and tone of voice
Brand hotspots	Priority points of intense customer connection and engagement with the brand
Brand intent	The vision and endeavor of the brand owner and management team to deliver a values-based brand experience to the customer
Brand loyalty	The ongoing customer trust that a brand enjoys
Brand owner	The ultimate legal owner of the brand (in the company)
Brand performance	The effectiveness and competitive power of the experience that the brand delivers
Brand personality	The style, attitude, and nature of how a brand behaves
Brand philosophy	The accepted understanding of the strategic place and power of a brand in achieving and sustaining successful business development
Brand portfolio	The range of brands that an organization possesses and markets
Brand position	The understanding that a brand commands about its particular customer relevance and competitive uniqueness
Brand positioning	The process of establishing or strengthening brand relevance in a defined market in order to develop and maintain a specific reputation and competitive position
Brand principles	The underlying truths and rules relating to the effective planning and achievement of brand growth and success
Brand resonance	The extent of the reach and impact of a brand in the market
Brand strategy	The plan that guides what the brand is to stand for in order to achieve relevance and competitive differentiation in the market
Brand value	The monetary value that can be attributed to a brand's worth at any given point in time due to its market power and appeal
Brand vision	The strategic intent of how the brand is expected to engage people and the market and impact on consumers' lives
Branding	The visual expression of a brand's innate idea, proposition, and uniqueness
C-suite	C-suite refers to the chief senior executives of an organization. Typically, their titles tend to start with the letter c, such as: chief executive officer (CEO), chief financial officer (CFO), chief operating officer (COO), and chief information officer (CIO)
Collective	The group of company stakeholders and expert advisors that is committed to, and is responsible for, the planning, design, promotion, and positioning of a brand

Expression	Explanation
Communication platforms	The range and variety of channels by which a brand message can be communicated
Competitive positioning	The different proposition that a company makes in the marketplace to achieve competitive advantage; the difference of a company's market offer relative to competitors
Consumer advocacy	The consumer's commitment to, and public support for, the brand
Consumption repertoire	The typical set of goods and services and brands that a customer consumes on a repeated basis
Core brand principles	The essential truths and rules relating to the effective planning and achievement of brand growth and success
Cross-integration	The inter-connection of different communication platforms to achieve enhanced coordination and market impact
Cultural norms	The set of standard beliefs, behaviors, or communications that characterize a societal or organizational culture
Culture	Organizational culture is the values and set of behaviors that are expressed, endorsed, and engrained among employees and suppliers. Brand culture is the commitment, over time, of people (in-company and in-market) to the brand
Customer touchpoints	The places and points in the buying process where the customer directly interacts with the company
Democratization	Achieving full availability and open access for the general public
Demographics	Socio-economic characteristics and statistical data relating to a population and its particular subgroups
Design execution	The creation of designs for identity development or brand and marketing communication
Emotional	The intangible experience that a brand provides that connects with customers at the nonphysical level
Emotional equity	The extent to which the intangible, nonphysical, emotional experience of a brand commands customer preference and ongoing loyalty
Empirical analysis	An analysis based on actual research observation or real-life experience as opposed to theory or logical deduction
Engagement	The extent to which a customer or an employee believes in and gets involved with the brand both physically and emotionally
Enterprise values	The standards, ethics, and codes of conduct and behavior prioritized and committed to by a business enterprise
Equity	The difference between what something is worth (an asset) and what is owed on it (debt and liabilities)
Functional	Physical attributes and benefits

(continued)

Expression	Explanation
Goodwill	The positive attitude toward the brand in the market; the extent to which it is held in high regard
Iconography	The use of visual imagery and symbols
Inherent values	The underlying, core values on which a brand is based
Internalization	The promotion and embedding of a brand's proposition and values internally across a company's employee base and systems
Legacy thinking	Knowledge, understanding, and perceptions that hark back to historic or previously accepted opinions, beliefs, or experiences
Licensor	The person or company that grants a license to another party (a licensee) to enjoy a limited right to use or market a brand
LMEs	Large and medium-sized enterprises
Macro level	High-level marketwide strategic concepts, developments, or trends
Management imperative	An absolute priority that management must address
Market positioning	The market sector or customer grouping for whom the brand is recognized to be highly relevant
Market segment	A specific category of customers within the market who have comparable needs and demands—they possess identical or similar requirements, expectations, or desires
Marketing collateral	The suite of design applications of the brand's identity for the purpose of presenting the brand and its product and service offer to the market
Marketing philosophy	The accepted understanding of the strategic place and power of marketing, and its component systems and tools, in achieving and sustaining successful business development
Millennials	Also known as *Generation Y*, millennials are people born from the mid-1970s to the mid-1990s whose birth cohort had reached early maturity by the year 2000—by the new millennium
Multiplier effect	Where a result is magnified due to the combined sharing and cross-fertilization of thinking, information, and expertise
Net Present Value	Net Present Value (NPV) analysis is used to help determine how much an investment, project, or any series of cash flows is worth. NPV is the value of all future cash flows (positive and negative) over the entire life of an investment discounted to the present
Niche market	A relatively confined, select, or specialist customer grouping or sector of the market
Norms	The set of standard beliefs, behaviors, or communications that characterize typical activity or normal practice
Nuance	A subtle difference in behavior, expression, or interpretation
Nuanced interaction	A sophisticated encounter that is highly subtle in its communication and relationship

Expression	Explanation
On-brand	To be in alignment with the brand values and proposition
Online socialization	The act and community-building effect of messaging and socializing via digital platforms
Paradigm	An accepted basic concept of theory, belief, or practice
Peer group	A primary, influencing social group of people who have similar interests, age, background, or social status
Performance-driving asset	A specific feature or attribute that is owned by a business that will distinctly increase the performance and profitability of the business in the market
Personalia	The biographical or personal details, preferences, or concerns associated with an individual or grouping
Pivot-product	A product invention that sets a whole new performance or service benchmark, creating a step-change in the standard of experience and expectation in the market
Points of difference	All and any ways in which the brand, its delivery, and consumption experience, is unique or different from competing brands
Portfolio	A catalogue or suite of brands, products, or services
Principles of branding	Underlying truths and rules relating to the effective application of branding as a system of communication and business growth
Proposition	What the brand stands for, believes about itself, and promises to the customer
Psychographic analysis	Analysis of consumer lifestyles via a qualitative methodology used to describe consumers on selected psychological attributes—typically applied to the study of personality, values, opinions, attitudes, interests, and lifestyles
Qualitative beliefs	The intangible, emotionally based understandings of the differential benefits and experience that a brand offers the market
Qualitative research	Research that is directed (moderated) but unstructured in order to determine perceptions, beliefs, feelings, emotional values, and deep-seated needs
Quantitative characteristics	The components of a brand that are product-focused in nature relating to what it is or what it functionally does
Rational values	Also known as functional values, these relate to physical, practical, nonemotional elements of a brand's offer
Rebranding	The act of replacing an existing corporate or product brand by planning, creating, and implementing an entirely new brand identity
Repositioning	The act of updating or changing the meaning and proposition of a brand for enhanced market relevance and competitiveness
Resonance	The extent of the market reach and impact of a business activity or brand innovation

(continued)

Expression	Explanation
Reverse-integration	The establishment of a systems connection and an open channel of communication between the company and the market, where the company mirrors current marketplace norms of activity and adapts to changing market behavior in real time
Royalty rate	A payment made by one party, the Licensee, to another party, the Licensor, for the use of the property or intangibles owned by the Licensor. A royalty rate is often expressed as a percentage of the revenues obtained by the Licensee when using the Licensor's property
Served market	A specific part of the total market that a company uniquely serves and in which it has a recognized brand presence
SMEs	Small and medium-sized enterprises
Social media narrowcasting	The highly targeted messaging and promotion of a brand via social media platforms to niche market segments, consumer groups, or individuals
Strategic intent	The vision and endeavor of the senior management team to achieve a particular business goal
Symbiotic relationship	A piggybacking type relationship where commercial benefits are mutually enjoyed due to collaborative sharing of vision, know-how, or market access
Tagline	A copywritten line that is incorporated into a brand identity to support and qualify a logo or a written brand communication
Tone of voice	The character and personality of a brand or a business that is conveyed through the use of words both spoken and written
Value-add	The total additional benefit that a brand provides to the customer
Value offer	The unique and total product value and customer experience that is promised or offered
Value proposition	The promise that a brand makes to its customer in terms of differential benefits, usage experience, and value for money
Value transaction	The exchange of value—via a monetary transaction—between company and customer, between brand and consumer
Values	What a brand or a business supports, promotes, and stands for as its essential ethics, priorities, and points of difference in both functional and emotional terms
Ways of working	Procedures and systems of internal organization that promote the development and maintenance of a companywide brand-centric culture

About the Author

Brian McGurk, *BA (Hons) Business Studies, Dip. Marketing*, has been working in strategic marketing and branding for about 30 years. He began his consulting career with PA Consulting Group and has founded and run three marketing and brand development agencies. His experience spans private and public sector organizations of all sizes and a highly diverse client base. He has established and led international brand teams at the cutting edge of business transformation and culture change. He has been a frequent commentator in the media and a speaker on brand experience and leadership at national and international levels. He is married with four adult children and lives in Dublin, Ireland.

Index

www.ingramcontent.com/pod-product-compliance
Lightning Source LLC
Chambersburg PA
CBHW061319220326
41599CB00026B/4949